The **Sewing Machine** Embroiderer's Bible

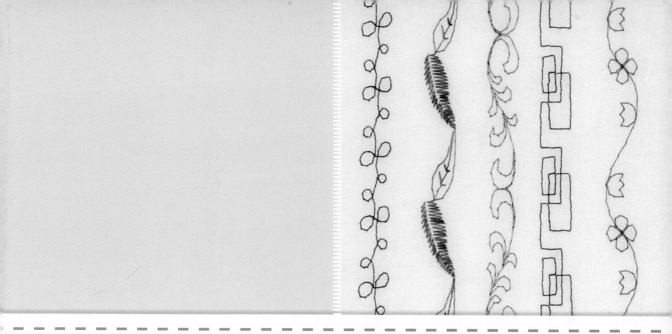

The **Sewing Machine**
Embroiderer's Bible

Get the most from your machine with embroidery designs
and inbuilt decorative stitches

Liz Keegan

ST. MARTIN'S GRIFFIN
NEW YORK

The Sewing Machine Embroiderer's Bible

A Quarto Book
Copyright © 2014 by Quarto Inc.
All rights reserved.

Printed in China. For information, address
St. Martin's Press, 175 Fifth Avenue, New
York, N.Y. 10010.

www.stmartins.com

Library of Congress Cataloging-in-
Publication Data Available Upon Request

ISBN: 978-1-250-04825-7

St. Martin's Griffin books may be
purchased for educational, business,
or promotional use. For information on
bulk purchases, please contact Macmillan
Corporate and Premium Sales Department
at 1-800-221-7945, extension 5442 or write
specialmarkets@macmillan.com

First Edition: August 2014

10 9 8 7 6 5 4 3 2 1

Conceived, designed, and produced by
Quarto Publishing plc
The Old Brewery
6 Blundell Street
London N7 9BH

QUAR.TMEB

Project Editor: Chelsea Edwards
Art Editor and Designer: Julie Francis
Photographers: David Garner and
    Simon Pask
Illustrator: Kuo Kang Chen
Copyeditor: Claire Waite Brown
Proofreader: Sarah Hoggett
Indexer: Helen Snaith
Art Director: Caroline Guest

Creative Director: Moira Clinch
Publisher: Paul Carslake

Color separation in Hong Kong by
Bright Arts Ltd

Printed in China by 1010 Printing
International Limited

Contents

Foreword

I have enjoyed all aspects of sewing
for years, but my real love is machine
embroidery, from using the decorative
stitches in my machine through to
full-scale embroideries.

I have never lost that magical feeling
when beautiful embroidery stitches out.
It started with my first embroidery machine
acquired some twelve years ago. I was
captivated from the word go!

My passion never waned and so I decided
I wanted to share it with others. Thus, *Flair
Machine Embroidery and Sewing Magazine*
was born in 2006 and I have compiled,
edited, and published *Flair* ever since.
However, it became apparent to me
that what was really needed was a
comprehensive reference book—a guide to
cover everything required for machine
embroidery in one place, complete with
explanation, clearly setting out methods
to obtain optimal results. So here it is! I
hope you find it interesting and informative.
My aim was to show the reader how to get
the best from their treasured sewing and
embroidery machine. I hope it answers
your questions, tells you how to avoid
mistakes, how to produce beautiful
pieces of work, and, most of all, how
to love embroidering.

Liz Keegan

About this book

Arranged into four separate chapters, all the vital aspects of machine embroidery are covered here. This book showcases the techniques used in machine embroidery for creating magnificent designs. From motif-style embroidery to ornate cutwork and exquisite heirloom creations, from simple appliqués right through to creating your own intricate lace, you'll find the instructions you need here. In addition to full embroidery designs, you can also explore the range of inbuilt decorative stitches your machine has to offer. They can add an attractive finish to many dressmaking and home-furnishing projects.

This book will provide you with all the know-how, tips, and tricks you need to machine embroider with ease and confidence. Information is also included on setting up and using your machine and software, selecting the correct tools and materials, and how to troubleshoot and look after your finished work.

Ideas file for each of the design techniques. These show examples of what can be achieved with the method.

The main characteristics of the technique are listed out here so that you can decide quickly if it's what you're after.

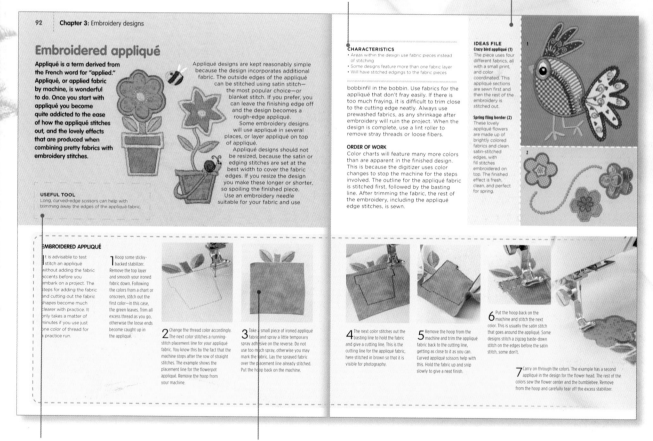

Helpful panels are featured throughout to offer tips to enhance your machine embroidery.

Large-format color photographs demonstrate the step-by-step techniques.

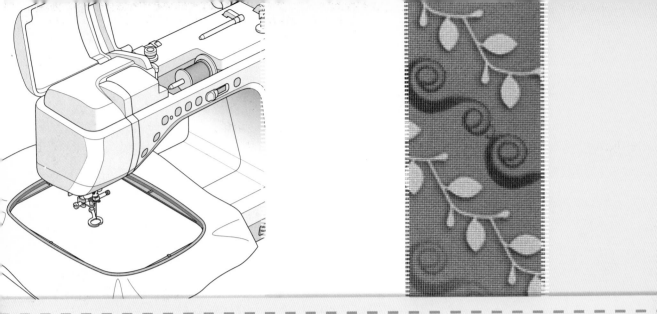

CHAPTER 1

Embroidery machines and computers

There are three main categories of embroidery machines that we cover in this chapter. Each one has a computerized element that interprets stitch data and sews out the embroidery design you have selected. Once you have exhausted the supply of embroidery design data that is built into your machine, you will want to explore other avenues and begin an embroidery design collection. This is where other methods of buying embroidery designs come into play. Learning simple computer procedures will allow you to build on your capabilities as you become more accustomed to the workings of your machine.

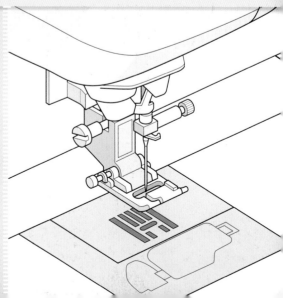

Embroidery machines

Although embroidery machines can be manufactured in different ways, they all accomplish the same thing—embroidery. You cannot do computerized machine embroidery unless you have a specialized unit or machine.

COMPARING EMBROIDERY MACHINES

The main areas of comparison between different embroidery machines are the amount of information the computer section can hold and the hoop sizes available. The hoop size and embroidery area within the hoop determine the size of the finished embroidery (see page 14).

Sewing/embroidery machine

These can range from very small sewing and embroidery machines with small hoops, through to the high end of the market and machines with large hoops and embroidery areas. The sewing machine is purchased with the machine embroidery capability, which can be a separate unit or have a carriage arm for hoops built into the main body, or have a carriage arm to attach to the main body that remains in position during normal sewing mode.

Sewing machine with optional unit

This is a higher-end sewing machine with embroidery capability. The main body of the sewing machine is sold as a singular unit and, should you want to embroider, you have the choice of buying an embroidery unit as a separate accessory.

Embroidery-only machine

A dedicated embroidery-only machine does not have a sewing function. These machines are very easy to use, because you don't have to navigate too many menus. Embroidery-only machines can be a very useful addition to the sewing room since you are not using your main sewing machine while embroidering.

Semi-industrial embroidery-only machine

Semi-industrial embroidery-only machines are manufactured for home use or for a small embroidery business run from home. These have more than one needle, depending on the brand, and so can accommodate more threads for quicker embroidery. The speeds at which they embroider are faster than home embroidery machines. They have a good range of hoop sizes and have useful accessories, such as a cap hoop.

Accessories

Accessories that are likely to be included with your purchase include a stylus for LCD screens, screwdriver, scissors, spare spool felts, spool caps of different sizes, spool nets, extra bobbins, and specialty feet.

MACHINE ANATOMY

Unpacking a sewing machine with an embroidery unit can seem a bit daunting, so over the next few pages we have detailed all the bits and pieces you use on a machine for embroidery, plus a few ideas for useful additions to your sewing box that will make life easier. One thing that cannot be stressed enough is not to be afraid! The machines are designed for use and they will not allow you to do things incorrectly, therefore you are unlikely to make a mistake and break it. If something is wrong, the machine will let you know by beeping or putting up an error message. Armed with this knowledge, start embroidering and love your machine.

The sewing/embroidery machine illustrated here is a mid-range machine, the Brother Innov-is V.5. Your machine may not have all the features or components listed, or it may have more. This book is as general as possible. There are so many brands and models of embroidery machines that it is impossible to be totally specific on these pages, so always refer to the manual for your own brand of machine. Your manual will be your best friend. Mark pages with sticky labels for quick reference at a later date.

Main body front

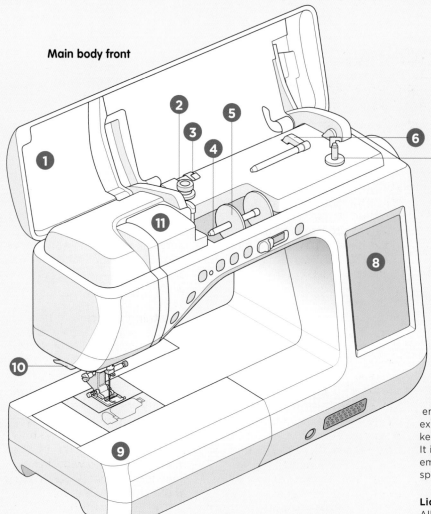

Extra spool pin and spool felt (6) This is used if a reel of thread is larger than will comfortably fit on the main spool pin. Some threads prefer to stand upright as they are wound on longer reels. Use this spool pin for winding the second thread when twin-needle sewing.

Bobbin winder (7) Prepare several bobbins before beginning large embroideries. Bobbins are not expensive, so buy some extras and keep them wound with bobbinfil. It is possible to wind bobbins during embroidery if you use the second spool pin.

Liquid crystal display (LCD) screen (8) All the information you need to embroider will be displayed here when you switch to embroidery mode. Use a stylus to touch the screen if your machine requires it.

Flatbed attachment (9) This is removed when embroidering. The embroidery unit slides into the resulting gap and is fitted to the machine.

Thread cutter (10) This is used for cutting threads after sewing and to put the thread around when using a lever-type needle threader.

Thread guide plate (11) When threading the upper thread, ensure that it is in the guides properly. Embroidery thread has sheen and so is slippery. It has to be gently pulled into these guides for even stitching.

Top cover (1) This is removed or lifted to thread the machine and wind the bobbin. It generally remains open during sewing.

Pre-tension disks (2) Pass the thread around the disk when winding a bobbin. Ensure that the thread is caught in the tension disks and wind bobbins for machine embroidery on slow. Bobbins must be wound evenly and you cannot wind thread onto an old bobbin. Begin with a properly wound bobbin using the correct thread, either bobbinfil underthread or, for decorative work, the same embroidery thread as the top thread.

Thread guide for bobbin winding (3) To wind a bobbin correctly, the thread must pass through this guide. Bobbin winding is different from threading, so follow the arrows carefully.

Spool pin and spool felt (4) The thread must sit on the spool pin properly and the thread needs to be able to move freely. Double-check to make sure it can. If the thread catches in the little nick on the thread top, turn it around so that the thread feeds in the other direction. Make sure that the thread doesn't get twisted around the spool pin. The thread felt is a piece of felt that sits at the bottom of a thread spool. If the thread tends to bounce around, a piece of felt is put on the spool.

Spool cap (5) A spool cap must be used to help the thread to wind off evenly and to stop the thread from moving around. There may be several sizes of spool cap in your machine's package; use the one nearest to your thread size. If necessary, use a thread net as well.

Operation buttons

Stop/start button (12) You don't use a foot controller when machine embroidering. You start and stop by pressing this button. Green is for "go," red is for "stop." You can use either the foot controller or the start and stop button for decorative stitching.

Reverse stitch button (13) Use this button to sew backward. Reverse stitch buttons need to be pressed in to make the machine sew in reverse.

Reinforcement button (14) Use this button with normal sewing to reinforce the beginnings and ends of seams. It sews a few stitches on the spot, or, if decorative sewing, will sew the last motif until it is complete and then the machine will stop.

Needle position up or down (15) Use this button to raise or lower the needle. It can be set to remain in either position, depending on your preference. If you set the needle to remain in the up position, remember to leave a longer thread tail, otherwise it unthreads itself, which can be most annoying.

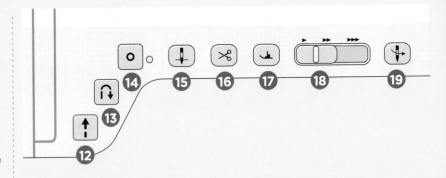

Thread cutter button (16) Use this to automatically cut the threads after normal sewing. It isn't used for machine embroidery. The automatic thread cutter, where there is one, is set inside the machine (see Machine settings, page 19).

Presser foot lifter button (17) Some machines have a presser foot button that is used to lift the presser foot. With other machines, you have to lift the pressure foot manually. For machine embroidery, you often have to manually use the double lift (see 22, below) to lift the presser foot high enough for the hoop to slide under.

Sewing speed controller (18) This is to slow the machine down or speed it up for sewing and decorative stitching. Some machines use this for machine embroidery speed as well. Most embroidery machines have the speed set inside the machine (see Machine settings, page 19).

Automatic threading button (19) Most machines have a threading system. This can mean pulling a lever or pushing a button. All threading systems can be overridden if you prefer.

Side view

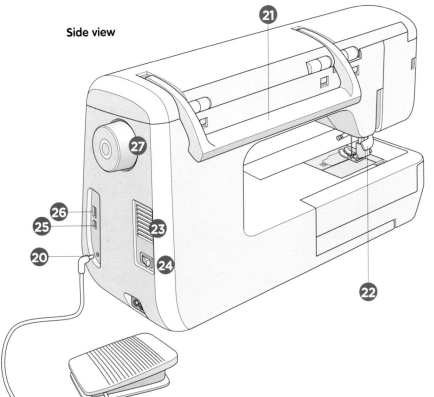

Connector for the foot pedal (20) The foot pedal is not used for machine embroidery, but can be used for decorative stitching.

Handle (21) Do not lift the machine or move it around once the embroidery unit is attached.

Presser foot lever (22) Use this to manually lift the presser foot. For a double manual lift, you have to lift it further than the first resistance for a bigger gap to slide your hoop under.

Air vent (23) Do not cover the air vent while embroidering. If the fabric falls over it, make sure there is a gap for air to circulate, especially with large embroideries containing thousands of stitches.

Mains power switch (24) Try not to turn off the machine when embroidering. If you do have to—for example after a needle break or thread jam—note the stitch number before turning off. When the machine has been turned on again, go forward to the stitch number and resume. If you have moved the beginning stitch away from the automatic center point while perfect positioning (see page 68), don't forget to save to the machine's memory before switching off, and restart from the design saved in the memory. The machine will remember that you moved the starting point and carry on where you left off.

USB port for direct link cable (25) This is the slot for the direct link cable from computer to embroidery machine.

USB slot (26) This is where you put the USB memory stick when loaded with embroidery designs.

Handwheel (27) Pull this toward you to raise and lower the needle or to make one stitch. You can also pull the bobbin thread up this way before putting the hoop on and embroidering your first stitches. Most machines do this automatically—but if the bobbin thread gets trapped under the plastic cover, the machine stops and says it isn't threaded correctly.

Embroidery card slot (not shown in this diagram). An embroidery memory card reader is an optional accessory for this machine and connects via the USB slot.

The needle area

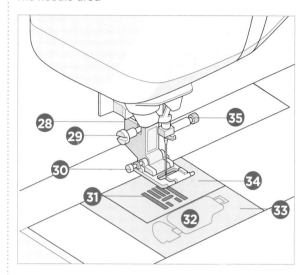

Presser foot holder (28) The presser foot holder needs to be removed to put the embroidery foot on. Ensure that the screw is done up properly around the embroidery foot and that the embroidery foot is on straight.

Presser foot holder screw (29) Make sure that the screw is tight around the presser foot holder or the embroidery foot.

Presser foot (30) A presser foot consistently holds the pressure on fabric as stitching takes place. The correct presser foot must be used for different types of stitching.

Feed dogs (31) These are in the up position for normal sewing and in the down position for machine embroidery. Check your manual to see if these are lowered automatically when selecting embroidery mode, or whether you have to manually lower them.

Bobbin cover (32) This is a clear plastic lid for the bobbin. You must put it on to ensure that the bobbin doesn't dance around in the bobbin case.

Needle plate cover (33) This needs to be removed regularly to clean out the bobbin area and the race. Machine embroidery creates a tremendous amount of lint, especially if you use cotton thread. Refer to your manual to find out how to do this and make it a regular occurrence.

Needle plate (34) Check the needle plate regularly and renew when necessary. If there is a slight burr, or a nick where a broken needle has caused damage, thread will continually catch and break.

Needle clamp screw (35) This needs to be tight around the needle. Embroidery is done at high speeds and the needle will fall out if it is not inserted correctly. Put the needle in with the flat top section facing away from you and insert as far as you can before tightening. Use the correct needle for your fabric when embroidering.

EMBROIDERY UNIT

Refer to the manual for specific directions for attaching the embroidery unit. The unit fits into the space left after the flatbed attachment has been removed. Some machines have the carriage arm attached and all you have to do is select embroidery mode for the carriage arm to slide into position.

Turn the power off before inserting an embroidery unit. You must tell the machine you wish to embroider by selecting embroidery mode after resuming the power. Tell the machine that you are removing the embroidery unit afterward by pressing the Remove Embroidery Unit button. The carriage arm on the removable embroidery unit will move back into park position before the unit is removed. Then turn the machine off and remove the unit.

Carriage (36) The carriage moves the embroidery hoop around while embroidering. Make sure that there is enough space around the machine for the carriage to move freely: if it knocks against a wall or other obstruction, damage will be caused to the timing and the machine. Only use a flat, stable, and sturdy surface, otherwise the speed of embroidering may make the machine vibrate. Check that fabric isn't caught up in any way before beginning to embroider.

Release button (37) The release button is located on the underneath or side of the unit. Use it to remove the unit after embroidery, after putting the carriage arm into the park position.

Hoop holders (38) The hoop must be inserted onto these correctly. If it isn't, a warning message will come up on the LCD screen.

Hoop lever (39) Not all machines have one of these. The lever needs to be pulled down to secure the hoop on the carriage. Check your manual to see how your hoop fits.

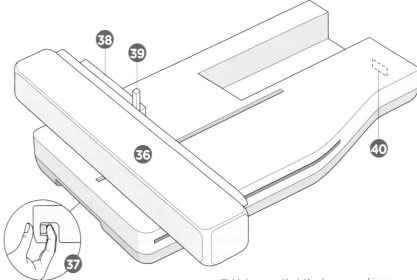

Embroidery connection unit (40) The embroidery unit needs to be inserted into the machine correctly. Once in position, the machine with unit attached should not be moved. However, if you really need to move it, use a hand at either end to keep it steady.

Embroidery hoops (41) Computerized machine embroidery requires a hoop to secure the work while embroidering. The hoop has two parts, made from rigid plastic, that fit onto the machine.

At least one hoop will be provided with every machine. Different brands of machine have particular sizes and shapes to fit their own machines. Embroidery hoops are not interchangeable between brands.

The top frame of the hoop needs to be inserted into the bottom frame correctly. Arrows are marked on the outer and inner frame to denote the correct insertion of top frame into bottom. The arrows must line up. There are also raised markings on the inner frame edges, top, bottom, center right, and center left, to assist with positioning fabric and for slotting in plastic templates. Always ensure that the screw is tight after hooping fabric.

The actual embroidery area within the hoop is smaller than the outer edges of the hoop to allow for the movement of the embroidery foot. Your machine will tell you which hoop to use when you choose a design. Always use the recommended hoop, which will be closest to your design size. If you try to

▼ Make sure that the hoop markings are in line to ensure that the top frame is inserted into the frame correctly.

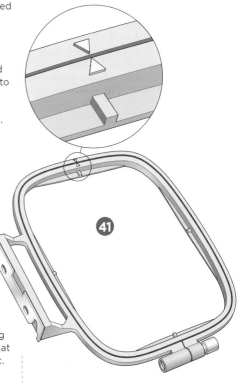

put in an embroidery design via an external medium that is larger in dimension than your largest hoop embroidery area, your machine will not recognize it.

Plastic templates (42) These are used for positioning embroidery. They lay inside the hoop and have cutout areas so that they can slot into the inner hoop markings.

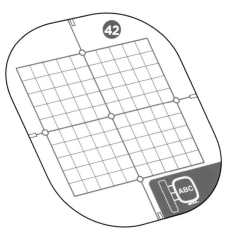

▲ When using a plastic template for positioning, ensure it is inserted into the hoop the right way up. This is because the embroidery area is not perfectly central.

Embroidery foot (43) This must be attached for machine embroidery using an embroidery unit. Use the one specified by your brand of machine.

USEFUL ADDITIONS TO YOUR SEWING BOX

Temporary adhesive spray (43) This spray, used for appliqué and quilting work, holds fabric temporarily in place while sewing. A very light spray is all you need. Keep the nozzle clear by washing it with warm water.

Curved appliqué scissors (44) These have a curved blade at the end and help with both appliqué and cutwork. Their long handles also make them good for trimming jump threads (when the embroidery moves from one area to another, leaving a long thread on the surface of the work). Always stop the machine before trimming jump threads.

Overlocker tweezers (45) These long tweezers are brilliant for catching broken pieces of thread from in and around the bobbin area, and if the thread breaks inside the thread guides. Switch your machine off before using them.

Thread stands (46) These are good for oversized cones and for metallic threads.

Cutting mat (47), quilting ruler (48), and rotary cutter (49) Use these to trim fabric after embroidery and for cutting quilting squares.

Magnifying glass Useful for cutting jump threads out of complicated embroidery designs if your machine doesn't do this automatically. These need to trimmed away during embroidery, between colors, otherwise they become trapped.

Marker pens—air- or water-removable (50) Useful for positioning embroideries. Always remove water-soluble marks before ironing, otherwise the marks will stay there forever.

Low-grade masking tape Use this when you want to position designs/templates on fabric but don't want to use a marking pen.

Using your embroidery machine

Now that you have familiarized yourself with the anatomy of your embroidery machine, it's time to get going. All embroidery machines have a selection of built-in embroidery designs to start you off and it is advisable to begin with these while you become accustomed to your machine.

GETTING STARTED
Work through this quick checklist to ensure you are ready to begin.

- Set up the embroidery unit by referring to your manual **(1)**.
- Switch on the sewing machine **(2)**.
- Lower the feed dogs manually, if your machine requires it.
- Put an evenly wound full bobbin of bobbinfil in and make sure the bobbin thread is pulled into the bobbin tension correctly.
- Attach the embroidery foot **(3)**.
- Put in an embroidery needle and ensure that it is fitted correctly **(4)**.
- Thread the machine with embroidery thread **(5)**.
- Prepare a hoop for embroidery with selected fabric and stabilizer, depending on your chosen design **(6)**.
- On a dual-purpose machine, select embroidery mode **(7)**.
- The machine will tell you it is going to move or calibrate the carriage. The carriage arm will move to its starting point **(8)**.

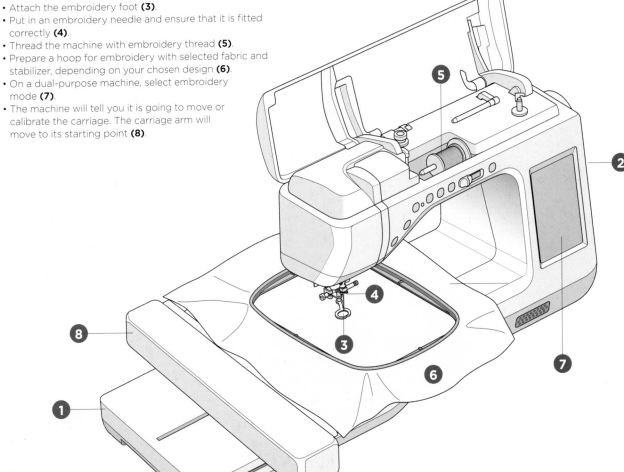

SELECTING AN EMBROIDERY

1 When you choose embroidery mode, the LCD screen will give you options: normal sewing, embroidery, or embroidery edit. Select embroidery to begin with.

3 Once you open a category or subcategory, the first selection will be for the middle-sized hoop for your brand. Where there is more than one page of designs to choose from, press the arrows back and forth. If your machine has larger or smaller hoops, the designs for these will be further on. Use fingertips or a stylus to touch the image of the design you want to embroider.

4 The embroidery design will appear on either the embroidery screen or the editing screen, depending on your machine. If your embroidery displays on the embroidery screen and you want to make changes, go to the editing screen (see page 21). If your embroidery displays on the editing screen and you are happy with it, go to embroidery. If any symbols are grayed out, it means they will not operate in the mode you are currently in. If you change modes, they will resume brightness and can be used.

2 You will be given a choice from all or some of the following. Sometimes these categories will have submenus. With this machine, the embroidery-mode icons are blue.

5 When you are ready to sew, press Embroidery (or OK on some machines). This is where all the information required to sew out the embroidery is displayed. The amount of information and functions available varies between brands.

In-built embroidery designs (1a–e) All machines have a selection of built-in embroidery designs so you can begin embroidering straight away. Some machines are shipped with a further supply on a separate CD-ROM.

Alphabets (2) A machine will feature a few built-in alphabets to allow you to add lettering to your designs. The ability to personalize embroidered items is one of the true joys of owning an embroidery machine. Each machine will have at least three fonts to choose from. You can make a word in embroidery mode or editing mode; however, if you want to alter character spacing or arrange the lettering, you need to do so in editing mode.

Patterns saved in the memory (or My Designs) (3) These are designs or design combinations that you want to save for future use. On a new machine, this section will be empty.

USB media (4) Search here for your USB memory stick. Some machines are shipped with a loaded memory stick of embroidery designs. You can also save your own designs to external media. This is also where you can open an embroidery card reader, as this accessory is connected via a USB port.

USB computer cable connection (5) This is where you open designs sent to the machine with a direct USB computer cable connection.

EMBROIDERY MODE

When you have entered embroidery mode, the screen shows you all the information you need to begin embroidering. Check that everything is correct before you begin. Any grayed-out keys are functions that are not available in this mode or for the embroidery selected.

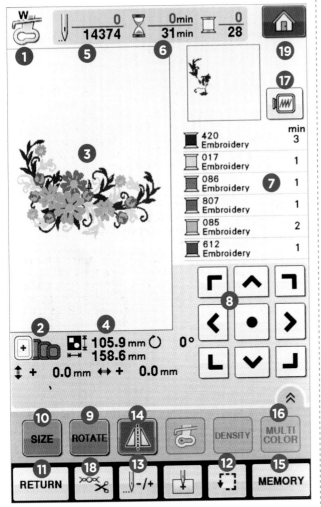

Presser foot symbol (1) The presser foot to be used. The foot will be labeled with a letter depending on the foot for your machine brand.

Hoop symbol (2) The boundary of the hoop. If your embroidery design exceeds the hoop embroidery area, the machine will tell you to change hoops. It will not allow you to embroider with a hoop that is too small. The hoop or hoops the design will not fit into are grayed out. If your hoop size needs to be altered, press the hoop icon to see the hoop sizes that your machine supports. Select the correct hoop for the design size (the closest above the embroidery design dimensions) and press OK.

Image (3) An image of the embroidery design. This is a small image in one color, or a detailed image in several colors. The clarity of the image depends on your machine.

Embroidery size (4) The dimensions of the embroidery will be in centimeters or millimeters, and is the size of the design both in height and width.

Stitch amount/counter (5) The total amount of stitches—this is also the stitch counter. This alters as you sew. As each stitch/thread color is complete, so the stitch counter decreases. The stitch counter is very useful if you turn off your machine and you need to know where to resume after turning it on again.

Time taken to sew (6) The time needed to sew the pattern, not allowing for stopping and thread changes. The time taken adjusts itself up or down if you alter the speed of your machine.

Color list and color number (7) The color list moves after each color is stitched, and puts the next color at the top of the list. The area to be stitched in the color is also shown. If you set your machine to one of the thread brand options listed internally, the thread color will also display a number or color name. Some machines are automatically set to the default thread for the company's own brand.

Note: On smaller machines, where the LCD screen isn't big enough to display all the information on one screen, there may be an arrow to find these other options.

Arrows (8) In embroidery mode, these keys move the embroidery starting point. Use them to move the hoop up or down, right or left, to ensure that the needle is over the center point of a template. They may be referred to as the positioning keys or the jog keys. On some machines, these may be dials on the front that you turn clockwise or counterclockwise.

Rotate (9) This may be in the embroidery screen, the editing screen, or both. The embroidery design can be rotated on the screen to alter its position. Sometimes a design will be smaller when turned 90 degrees, so you can use a smaller hoop. If you rotate a large design 45 degrees, you may find that the hoop you were originally using becomes too small, since designs are often wider when on an angle. If so, alter your hoop size.

Size (10) Press this to alter the size of the design. The total recommended amount is 20 percent either up or down. Small square boxes will have arrows and options for making the design wider, narrower, taller, or shorter, or there will be percentage keys for each direction. The choice of reducing or increasing equally in all directions will also be available. Some machines use knobs for the alterations that work when this key is selected.

Return (11) Press to return to the embroidery selection page if you change your mind about the design you have chosen. You may be asked if you want to delete the pattern. Press OK.

Trial (12) A very good key to use. When you touch it, the machine will do a trial of the area where the embroidery is to be sewn. If you have a large piece of fabric, or an item of clothing, this quick pre-run will allow you to see if any fabric is caught up.

Forward/back (13) Use to go forward or backward in a design. You can go in either direction by jumping stitches or by thread colors. This is very handy if your thread breaks. Select this icon, re-thread the machine, and go backward a few stitches. This way there is no gap. If you have inadvertently put the wrong color on and you want to go back to the beginning of the color to sew over it with the right color, use the thread color keys to go back a color. If you want to sew just the outline of a design, which is usually the last color, jump through all the colors until you have just the black remaining and stitch out the black only.

Horizontal mirror image (14) Use this key to alter the design so that it is mirror imaged. Some machines have horizontal and vertical mirror imaging.

Memory (15) Use this key to save a design to the machine's memory. The memory in a machine has a stitch capacity. If it is full, the machine will tell you to delete one before a new one can be saved.

Multicolor (16) Use this key to alter character or letter colors. When adding a word or characters, an embroidery machine automatically sets the default as black or follows on from the last color stitched in a design.

Image view (17) View a sample of how the stitched embroidery will look by using this key.

Cut/tension (18) This will take you to the top tension and jump thread cutting operation keys in machine settings. These are automatically set for embroidery, but can be overridden.

Home key (19) Use this key to return to the main home selection page to choose between sewing, embroidery, and embroidery edit.

MACHINE SETTINGS

It is possible to change the settings in the Set Menu or Embroidery Settings, or by pressing a tools icon. The settings will differ between machines, but may include some of the following:

Screen You can alter the language displayed on the screen as well as the color of the display and its brightness.

Sewing speed You can choose between the slowest and fastest speeds your machine will stitch at, with increments in between.

Upper tension To increase or lower the upper thread tension. It is automatically set to optimum tension, but this will override the default setting.

Bobbin thread You can set the amount of bobbin thread you want left on the bobbin before receiving an insufficient bobbin thread message.

Sounds on or off You can turn the sounds off on some machines, although this is not necessarily a good idea since sounds will alert you to a problem.

Thread brand Set the thread/color display so that it shows different thread brands, from one brand in smaller embroidery-only machines onward. Some machines will allow you to create a custom thread table.

Format If your machine requires you to format a memory card or USB stick, you will do so here. If your media requires reformatting, you need to find the format area to restore to default. If you reformat any media, you will erase all embroidery designs stored—so make a backup before reformatting.

Thread cutter If your machine has an optional jump thread cutter, the settings will allow you to switch it on or off.

Presser foot height Some machines will allow you to adjust the embroidery presser foot height in millimeters for embroidering on different thicknesses of fabric.

Restore to default The machine will restore itself to all factory settings.

ERROR MESSAGES

Error messages appear on the screen when something is wrong. The machine may not start because of an error, or will stop itself automatically. Take notice of these and put right whatever is wrong before resuming embroidery. Touch the error message to cancel it after you have rectified the problem. A machine's manual will include a list of error messages and what they mean. Here are some examples of common error messages.

ERROR MESSAGE SHOWN	SOLUTION
INCORRECT HOOP ATTACHED	The hoop you have put on the machine is not large enough for the embroidery selected. Change your hoop. Some machines require you to change your hoop within the menu in the displayed hoop icon; others allow the sensors to recognize the different hoop.
HOOP NOT ATTACHED CORRECTLY	Take the hoop off and put it on again, this time ensuring it is correctly positioned.
LOWER PRESSER FOOT	The presser foot needs to be lowered.
NEEDLE BROKEN	Take out the needle and replace it with a new one. The machine will sense if a needle is bent and display this message.
THREAD BROKEN	Take out the upper thread and re-thread the machine. It is better to re-thread completely. If this message persists even after re-threading several times, check the bobbin thread, since not all machines can tell the difference between the problem being with the top thread or the bobbin sensors. The bobbin thread might have a tail that is annoying the bobbin sensors, or it may have come out of tension or snapped.
INSUFFICIENT BOBBIN THREAD	This message may come up when the bobbin thread is about to run out.
INSUFFICIENT MEMORY	There is not enough space in the machine's memory to save the specified embroidery. Delete saved designs and try again.

EDITING MODE

In this screen you can move designs, add lettering, alter and repeat designs, as long as the combination fits into the embroidery area of your hoop.

You cannot alter your design in embroidery mode. To alter a design combination you have saved, you must return to the editing screen. Once you are happy with the alterations you have made, select the embroidery screen to stitch out.

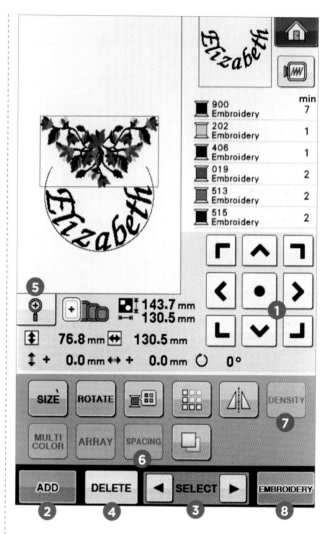

Arrows (1) Here, the arrow keys are used to move a single design or several designs, including words, to arrange a combination. Use Select to move or edit the part of the design you want. The center key will move the design back into the center of the hoop.

Set (not shown in this screen) As you add a design to the editing screen, you need to press the Set key. This confirms that you are keeping your choice and gives you all the options to set/arrange the design. As you bring new designs into the layout, press Set after each addition. The Set key is also used to rearrange each selection individually in the layout after selection.

Add (2) Use this to build up your design by bringing in a second design or word. After you have selected the embroidery, press this key to go back to the home page selection and choose another to merge with the first. Some machines require that you press the home icon or the embroidery selection icon.

Select (3) Use this to choose a design from the screen to alter, move, or delete.

Duplicate (not shown in this screen) This key is used to repeat a design to save you having to go back to the home screen to bring it into an arrangement. The design has to be selected before duplicating.

Delete (4) On some machines, this is indicated by a trash can icon. If only one design is on the screen, select it and delete it. To delete a design from a combination, press Select and follow through with the arrows until the embroidery you want to delete is selected, then press Delete.

Magnify (5) Some machines have a key to magnify the embroidery on screen.

Arrange (not shown in this screen) If your machine has one, use this key to arrange lettering in different configurations.

Character spacing (6) This key is used to rearrange your letters and change the space between characters.

Density (7) Use this key when altering the density of characters, frames, and some designs. You will be allowed to have up to 20 percent fewer or 20 percent more stitches. This only works if the key is bright on the screen. If it is grayed out, try pressing Select. If it stays grayed out, this option is not available.

Embroidery (8) Use this key to go to the embroidery screen when you have finished editing. Your edited designs will now be in embroidery mode for you to stitch out.

Uninterrupted embroidery (not shown in this screen) Use this key if you want to sew the whole selected design out in one color.

Function (not shown in this screen) Touch this key to display all the keys on this screen.

EXAMPLE OF COMBINING LETTERING AND DESIGN WITH DUPLICATION AND ROTATION

1 Select a font from the embroidery edit menu and type your chosen word. Arrange the lettering by selecting Array. The sample shows an arc.

2 A design is added to the lettering. Bring a new design in by selecting Add, then the Set key. The red box around the design shows that it is selected.

3 If you want to sew the design as it is, select Embroidery and the embroidery screen opens up with the combined design on the screen. Now you are ready to embroider.

4 The combined embroidery has been taken back into editing mode. The main embroidery design is duplicated and rotated to mirror the first. The finished combination is put into embroidery mode for you to stitch out.

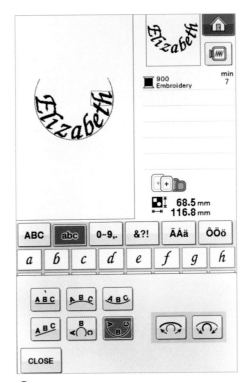

❶

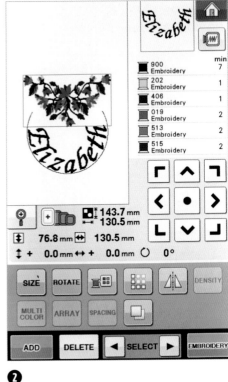

❷

❸

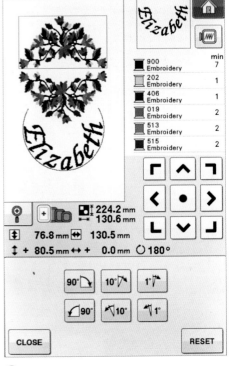

❹

EXAMPLE OF REPEATING AND MIRRORING A DESIGN

1 A design is brought into the editing mode and Set. It is rotated 90°. A second design, a repeat of the first, is brought in. The second design is Set and then rotated 90°.

2 The repeated design is mirrored horizontally and moved inside the hoop area with the arrow keys. Note the design being worked with has a red box around it to show that it is selected.

3 The edited and combined design is sent to the embroidery screen, ready to sew.

4 The Basting key is used if you want to add a basting line around your embroidery to further secure fabric to stabilizer. Not all machines have this function. The color black appears at the top of the color list as an extra color. The extra color is the color for the basting stitches. You can change the color. Bear in mind that adding basting to the outside of the embroidery may mean that you need to move up a hoop size.

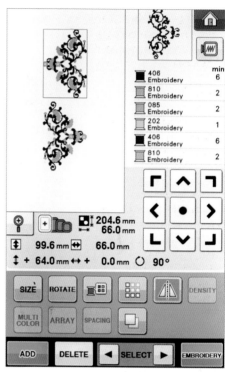

❶

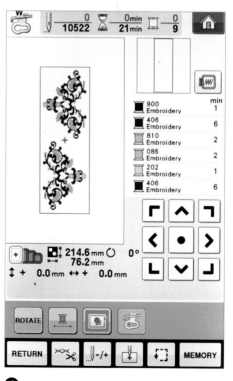

❷

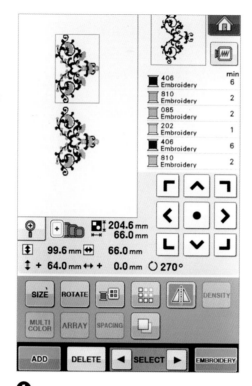

❸

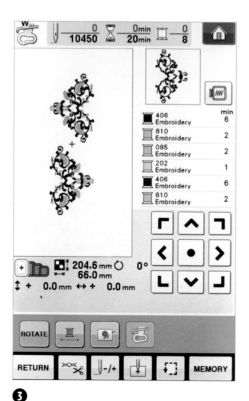

❹

Choosing and transferring designs

When choosing machine embroidery designs, you must be aware of the file format that your machine will accept, and understand which methods of transferring designs are suitable for your machine.

FILE FORMATS

A file format is designated by the file extension given at the end of the file name. This shows how the stitch file is saved. When an embroidery design is digitized, it is saved into a format suitable for specific embroidery machines. For example, Brother embroidery machines use a .PES format, Bernina machines an .ART format, and so on. Some machines will read and recognize only one of the formats from the panel below; others will be able to read and recognize several. If you are unsure, check your manual or consult with the machine's manufacturer and dealership to find out exactly which format(s) the machine will support. It is important that you do not change the extension, otherwise the file will not open in your machine.

Whether you buy your embroidery design on a card, a USB memory stick, a CD-ROM, or as a download from the Internet, you need to ensure

that you buy the design in a format that is suitable for your machine. If you buy a design that is machine-specific the format will automatically be correct, so a design card for a Brother machine will be loaded with the correct format for Brother machines. If you buy designs from the Internet, however, you will need to choose the right format or have software that can convert your purchased format into one suitable for your machine.

Multi-format

A multi-format design or design set will have many formats included; check to make sure that your format is one of them.

Converting formats

If you own software that is capable of converting formats from one to another, you don't have to buy a format specific to your machine. The design can be purchased in one format and converted to another using the software.

DESIGN SIZE

When choosing embroidery designs, always make sure that you check the dimensions of the design. If the design size is larger than your largest embroidery hoop, your embroidery machine may not recognize the design when it is transferred over. Some machines will allow you to locate and resize the design in the editing screen, but most machines will reject it.

COMMON FILE FORMATS

Bernina	.PEC, .PES, .ART, .EXP
Brother/Babylock	.PES
Husqvarna Viking	.VP3, .SHV, .HUS
Pfaff	.PCS, .VIP, .VP3
Elna	.EMD
Janome	.SEW, .JEF, .JEF+
Singer	.XXX

▶ Underneath the design it will state the finished dimensions. Make sure this does not exceed your largest hoop size.

Cherry Blossom Border (D7072)
Size: 6.00 x 1.74in (152.4 x 44.2mm)
Stitch count: 11091

METHODS OF TRANSFERRING EMBROIDERY DESIGNS

There are various ways of getting embroidery designs onto your embroidery machine, the most widely used of which are listed below. Consult the machine's manual to see which methods it supports, and find the easiest for you.

TRANSFER METHOD	ADVANTAGES	DISADVANTAGES
Embroidery design card or embroidery design USB memory stick Embroidery design sets from machine manufacturing companies are the easiest to use, but also the most expensive. These will insert into a specific part of your machine and the embroidery designs will load when you select the correct icon on the machine's screen—the machine's manual will indicate which screen icon opens embroidery cards or USB memory sticks.	• Easy to use • Easy to buy • Wide selection available for all machines • No computer knowledge required	• Expensive • Not interchangeable between machine brands
Wireless capability The newest embroidery machines use wireless transfer of the embroidery design from computers and tablet, directly to the machine. The design is then saved into the internal memory of the embroidery machine.	• Easy to transfer designs to machines	• Dependent on a wireless Internet connection • Computer/tablet knowledge required
USB memory stick Embroidery designs in the correct format can be copied or dragged onto a USB memory stick from a computer. The memory sticks can be machine-specific or bought from a computer supplies stockist: check your manual to see which type your machine requires. Insert the memory stick into the embroidery machine and select the memory stick icon to see the designs on the LCD screen—the machine's manual will indicate which screen icon opens USB memory sticks. Some machines require that a USB memory stick be formatted before use. To do this, insert the stick into the machine and follow the on-screen instructions. Once formatted, the memory stick creates a folder for embroidery files; make sure that all the embroidery designs put onto the memory stick are put inside this folder, otherwise the machine will not be able to read them.	• Easy to use • Can store a large number of embroidery designs • Can download designs directly onto the USB memory stick • Can edit in software and save the edited design to a USB memory stick without having to save to a computer first	• Basic computer knowledge essential • Machine-specific USB memory sticks are initially expensive • Are not infallible

TRANSFER METHOD	ADVANTAGES	DISADVANTAGES
Direct cable embroidery A cable runs from a USB port on the embroidery machine directly to a USB port on the computer. An embroidery design is then stitched out using the direct link, so the computer must be connected to the embroidery machine in order to work.	• Easy to see the embroidery design sewing on the computer screen • Easy to open embroidery designs stored on your computer • Embroidery edits can be completed on the computer screen	• Needs to link directly to a computer to embroider • Need to install provided software • Basic computer knowledge required
Direct cable transfer A cable runs from a USB port on the embroidery machine directly to a USB port on the computer, and the embroidery design is transferred onto the machine. The embroidery machine comes up on the computer as an external drive. The PC Link screen within the embroidery machine is opened and the design is then sent from the computer. The embroidery design is then saved into the memory within the machine. The computer can then be disconnected and the design remains in the machine until it is deleted.	• Easy to use • Embroidery design loads into the machine from the computer instantly	• Basic computer knowledge required • Can quickly exceed the built-in memory capacity of the embroidery machine
Direct cable transfer—older machines Machines that are a few years older require machine-compatible software to enable the direct cable transfer. The transfer is completed by opening the PC Link screen in the software and selecting the Send to Machine option on the top toolbar.	• Easy to use • Embroidery edits can be completed in the software and transferred without having to save them first	• Machine-compatible software required • Basic computer knowledge required • Can quickly exceed the built-in memory capacity of the embroidery machine
Compact flash card Some machines use a flash card to transfer embroidery designs. The flash card needs to be put into the machine to be formatted before use. During formatting, one or several folders will appear, depending on the storage capacity of the card. Embroidery designs need to be inside one of these folders in order for the machine to read them.	• Easy to use • Can store a large number of embroidery designs • Can download embroidery designs directly onto the flash card • Can edit in software and save the edited design to a flash card without having to save to a computer first	• Basic computer knowledge essential • Not infallible • May need to purchase a separate USB flash card reader if the correct port is not on your computer • Need to be machine formatted before use • Will need a PCMCIA ATA adapter (shown left) to put the flash card into the machine.

◀ Compact flash adaptor and card. The compact flash card is slotted into the adaptor and then both are inserted into the embroidery machine.

TRANSFER METHOD	ADVANTAGES	DISADVANTAGES
Memory card reader/writer This is a company- and machine-specific card reader/writer used with software to transfer embroidery designs. The design is opened on a computer in the software that came with the embroidery machine and, once opened, written to the memory card. The memory card is then inserted into the machine and the design is stitched out. Memory cards do not have a large capacity and often only one design at a time can be stored.	• Company-specific	• Basic computer knowledge required • Small capacity • Software required to write to them • Cannot be used in different brands of embroidery machine • Need to be purchased with software as an optional accessory
Embroidery design CD from external drive Not many machines can read directly from a CD-ROM. If your machine uses an optional CD-ROM drive, you can read the CD from your machine without having to put the embroidery design into the machine's memory. Insert the disk into the drive and connect the USB cable from the drive to the embroidery machine. Select the CD icon on the machine and choose your embroidery design.	• Wide design-set choice available on CD-ROM • Easy to use • Connects directly to the machine	• Usually an optional accessory • Limited machines use CD-ROM • Your format must be on the CD-ROM
Embroidery design CD from computer Mostly, embroidery designs from a CD-ROM are copied from the disk first and stored on a computer. Load the embroidery design CD into the computer and open the disk to view the embroidery files loaded on it. Choose the designs that you want to use, ensuring that you use the right format. Copy those designs onto your computer to be stored for later transfer to your embroidery machine, using one of the above methods.	• CDs rarely break if stored correctly. If marks prevent a CD from loading properly, use eyeglass cleaner to polish the CD and remove light scratches. • Reasonably priced and wide selection of designs are available • Many are multi-format, so can be used in most home embroidery machines.	• Some computer knowledge is essential • You have to know your format and be able to copy the right file of embroidery designs into your computer or onto your USB memory device • Don't always have hard-copy templates included, so you have to have access to a printer

Computer basics

Basic computer skills are all you really need to know for machine embroidery. Keeping your designs named and stored properly in ordered subfolders, within an Embroidery Designs folder, will make them easy to find and save you time.

When using a computer for embroidery for the first time, set yourself up as a new user and keep all your embroidery designs in one place, in a named folder within Documents. If there are too many files and folders on a family-used screen, you can easily lose track. As a new user you will have an empty user space, which makes life much simpler. To set yourself up as a new user, refer to your computer's Help section.

MAKING A FOLDER

In order to organize and keep track of your embroidery designs, you will need to create a folder in Documents. The example uses the Windows 7 operating system. The instructions are similar for previous versions. Open your computer under your user name.

1 Left click on the Start menu Windows icon at the bottom left-hand corner of the screen.

2 Select Documents.

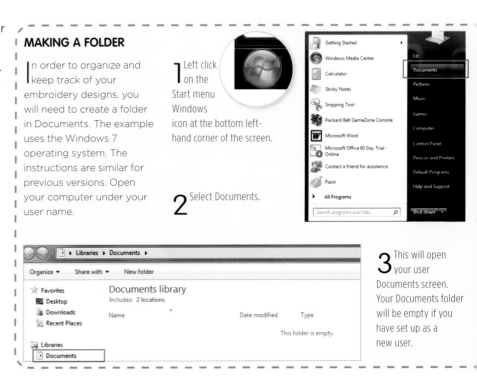

3 This will open your user Documents screen. Your Documents folder will be empty if you have set up as a new user.

RENAMING FILES

All work with embroidery designs will now be completed inside this folder. You can also use the same method to make subfolders inside Embroidery Designs, which will help you to keep organized. When naming files or folders, only use uppercase/lowercase letters and numbers. You can use spaces, but the computer may not allow you to use symbols such as slashes or asterisks, or some punctuation marks, resulting in an error message. This error message can be frustrating, so it is better to avoid using any of them altogether. You cannot name or rename a folder or file while it is open or open in another program.

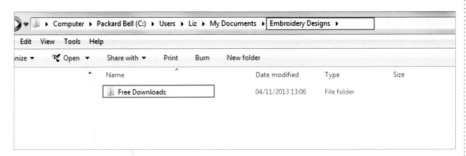

A subfolder called Free Downloads has been made within the Embroidery Designs folder.

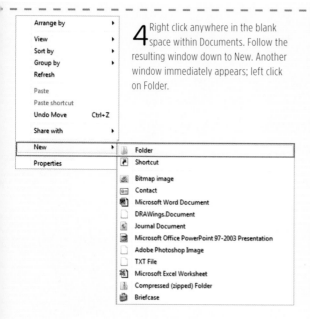

4 Right click anywhere in the blank space within Documents. Follow the resulting window down to New. Another window immediately appears; left click on Folder.

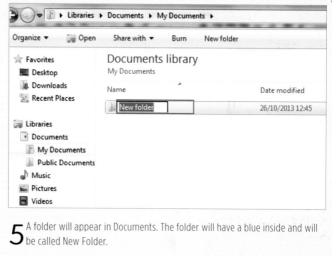

5 A folder will appear in Documents. The folder will have a blue inside and will be called New Folder.

6 To rename the folder, follow the above steps and select Rename instead of New. This highlights the new folder and you use the keyboard to rename. Call this folder Embroidery Designs. Use the same method whenever you want to rename an embroidery design or folder.

HIGHLIGHTING, DRAGGING, AND DROPPING

1 To put loose embroidery designs into subfolders, hold the embroidery design by left clicking on it and holding the left click down. This highlights the embroidery design in a light shade of blue. You have now selected the design.

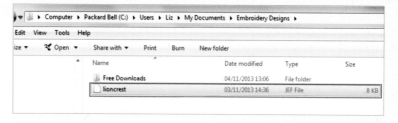

2 Keep the left-hand side of the mouse down and drag the embroidery design into the subfolder called Free Downloads. You can see the design is being moved as the screen tells you this is happening. This is called dropping. Dragging and dropping is an easy way to move files from a folder into a subfolder.

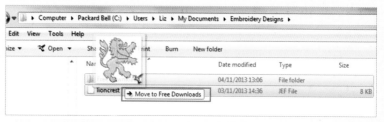

Downloading designs from the Internet

Single embroidery designs and design sets are easily downloaded from the Internet. If you are unsure of the process, use free designs to practice downloading—then if you do lose track of them on the computer, you haven't lost any money. Begin buying once downloading and saving have been mastered.

When buying embroidery designs from the Internet, you need to know your machine's required file format (see page 24). When you are asked which format you require, select it from the options, usually in a drop-down box. A multi-format design set will list the formats included, so check first to make sure that yours is there, since the formats included can vary between sites.

REGISTRATION

The first thing you need is an email address. All sites require this when you register to make an account or make an individual purchase. You will also need a payment method.

Digitizers and embroidery malls use different shopping cart software, so not every site is exactly the same. Some sites will ask you to register to create an account and your purchases will be in the download section of your account. Others will send you to a link from which you download the design. Others will send you an email with a link to the download. The actual downloading process remains the same, whatever link you are using. The download can be either a single file or a compressed folder. Most embroidery sellers will have a FAQ section. Read this carefully before making a purchase.

DOWNLOAD METHODS

Downloading using the Save As command allows you to download to a specified folder on your computer, and also lets you rename the download as you save it. Using the Save command, on the other hand, will download to a destination on your computer called Downloads. If you download using Save, you locate your download in the Downloads folder. However, you have to rename it and move it to your Embroidery Designs folder afterward.

Using the Save As command is the easiest and most organized system. Many embroidery designs or design sets are only named with code. You can rename the download before it comes into your computer, which makes organization easier.

DESIGN VARIETY

The choice of embroidery designs available from the Internet is vast. Whatever you wish to embroider you can be sure there will be an embroidery digitized that will be suitable. Shown opposite are a variety of embroideries, from denser flowers to line-drawn birds to homely tea cup designs. These are a small selection from one embroidery site alone. Keep a list of your favorite sites and all your user names and passwords. There are so many that you can forget and waste time trying to remember what embroidery selection was available from which site. Worse still, the site won't let you in because you have registered on a previous occasion and you are using incorrect details to try and access it again. Download free designs to test them out before buying. Any reputable machine embroidery sites or digitizers are proud of their skill and will allow you to download free designs to try out.

DOWNLOADING YOUR DESIGN

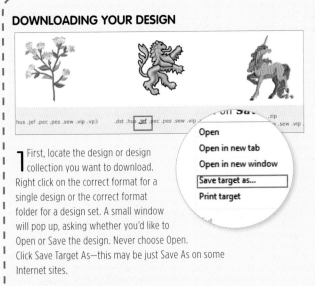

1 First, locate the design or design collection you want to download. Right click on the correct format for a single design or the correct format folder for a design set. A small window will pop up, asking whether you'd like to Open or Save the design. Never choose Open. Click Save Target As—this may be just Save As on some Internet sites.

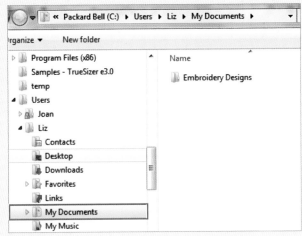

2 A new window will pop up, asking where you want to save your free design. Choose your Embroidery Designs folder.

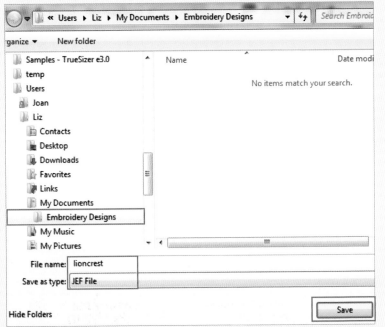

3 Double click on the Embroidery Designs folder. You will see that it is empty until you put embroidery designs into it. Note that the wording alters as you open the Embroidery Designs folder. The format is shown with the name of the design—in this case, lioncrest.jef. It is at this point that you can rename the download if desired.

4 Click Save. Your embroidery design will begin downloading. When it has finished downloading, a new box appears at the bottom of the computer screen. The new box tells you that the download has completed.

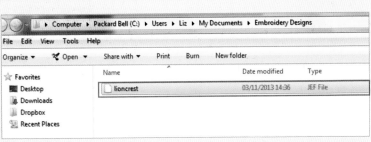

5 Click on Open Folder. The design is now downloaded and ready to be transferred to the embroidery machine (see pages 24–27).

UNZIPPING FILES

Sometimes a collection of designs will be saved in what's known as a zipped or compressed file. Unzipping the compressed folder allows you to get to the folder's contents, and Windows Vista and Windows 7 have in-built programs to unzip compressed files.

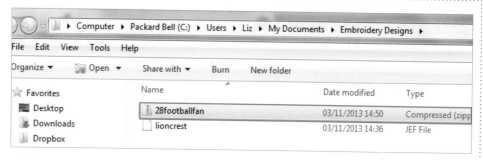

1 To download a zipped folder, follow the usual process (see page 32). The zipped folder in the Embroidery Designs folder has a little gold zip on. It is named 28 footballfan.

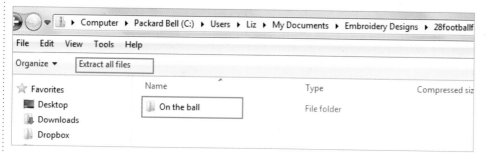

2 Very quickly left double click on the folder. You will notice that the toolbar naming has altered. Along the top of the window should be the words Extract All Files; you can see that the contents of the compressed zipped folder is a subfolder called "on the ball."

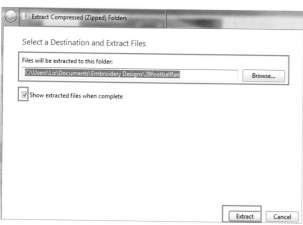

3 Left click on Extract All Files and another window will come up in the middle of the screen. This is the Extraction Wizard. Note that it's still asking to save the designs in your Embroidery Designs folder. It will create a new, unzipped version with the same name. Uncheck the Show Files option. Left click Extract. The window will show the progress of the extraction and, once it's complete, the window will disappear.

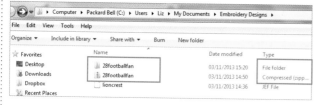

4 On returning to the Embroidery Designs folder you will notice two different subfolders, each with the same name of 28 footballfan (in this example). One will be labeled 28 footballfan Compressed Zip Folder (the original download), and the other, called 28 footballfan Folder, is the one the computer automatically created during unzipping. This is where you'll find your embroidery designs.

BACK UP YOUR DESIGNS
Make a backup of downloaded designs by copying them to a USB memory stick. Some sites will allow you to download files again should your computer crash. Others won't.

CORRUPTED DOWNLOAD?
Corrupted downloaded files will refuse to unzip properly. If this happens, close down the Internet browser, reload, open a new window, and try again. The problem is often rectified with a new download.

Copying designs to external hardware

Any external device connected to your computer from outside is known as external hardware or external drive. The external hardware becomes the medium for transporting embroidery designs from the main computer to the computer inside the embroidery machine.

The basics of copying designs to external hardware are the same, regardless of the form the hardware takes.

COPYING TO A USB MEMORY STICK OR FLASH CARD

If your embroidery machine requires a company-specific USB memory stick, it is likely to have some designs already installed for you to use. If it is a blank USB memory stick or flash card, it will be empty.

If your embroidery machine has the ability to read designs directly from a USB memory stick or a flash card, the copying process is relatively easy. Check with the manufacturer which USB memory stick or flash card is compatible with the machine.

Formatting

If you have a new USB memory stick or flash card, insert it into the embroidery machine to see if it needs to format it before it is ready for use. Once inserted, if the message Ready to Format appears, follow the onscreen instructions to format your hardware or make it ready for use. For example, with Janome MC 12000 embroidery machines, the first time a USB or flash card is inserted it will be automatically formatted by following the onscreen prompts. In doing so, an embroidery folder labeled EMB is made with

internal subfolders labeled Embr1, Embr2, etc.—how many there are depends on the size of the memory. The .JEF or .JEF+ design files must be inside one of these Embr folders for the sewing machine to find it.

Copying

Plug the USB memory stick into a USB slot on your computer, or insert the flash card into the slot: if your computer does not have a flash card slot, you can buy an external flash drive that plugs into a USB port. If you are using a laptop, USB ports will be near your CD/DVD drive. If you are using a desktop, there will be one on the tower or, if you have a standalone monitor, it is likely to be on the back of the monitor.

SELECTING MULTIPLE DESIGNS

You can send a whole collection of designs by highlighting them all, left clicking, and sending them all in one go. While holding the left-hand side of the mouse down, put the cursor at the top left-hand corner and drag it across as many files as you want to send, still holding the left side down. When all the files you want are highlighted, let the mouse go. The files will have a blue background. Right click to send them all to the external device or Documents folder.

Now the embroidery design/s are either on your external

COPYING DESIGNS TO A USB STICK

In this demonstration a Disgo USB memory stick is used, but the process is the same for stick or flash card.

1 Insert your USB stick into the USB port. A window of options will pop up. Left click Open Folder to View Files; a window will then display everything stored on the hardware (nothing if it is new)—in this case, an EMB folder formatted for a Janome embroidery sewing machine. The memory stick has opened in Drive (E:) and is labeled with the manufacturer's name. Different computers will open hardware in different drives. Minimize the window by clicking on the center open square in the top right-hand corner. This brings Drive (E:) down to the bottom of the computer screen.

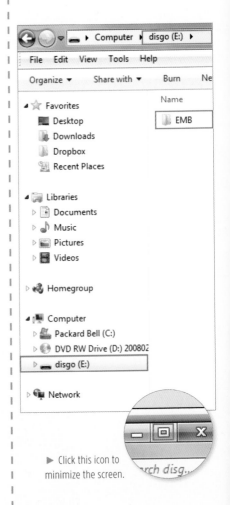

▶ Click this icon to minimize the screen.

2 Now go back to the Start menu and open Documents in a new window: you can have several windows open at a time. Double click on the Embroidery Designs folder to open it.

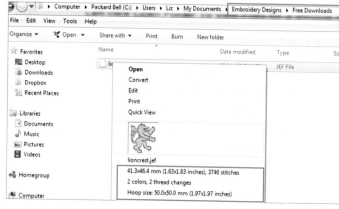

3 Inside Embroidery Designs is a subfolder called Free Downloads. On opening Free Downloads, the lioncrest.jef design can be seen. Right click on the file to see the list of options, including the properties of the embroidery design. This computer has embroidery software installed, which is why you can see a small picture of the embroidery design. Check the design dimensions. If the size is larger than your biggest hoop, it will not register in your machine.

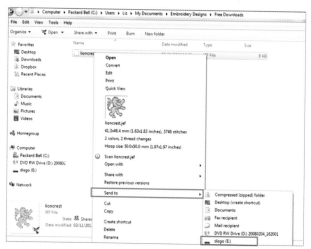

5 Go back to the small yellow folder at the bottom left-hand of your computer screen and hover the cursor over the folder. Two faint, smaller windows appear. One is your USB memory stick, the other is your Embroidery Designs folder. Click on the USB folder and the window maximizes. You can now see that the lioncrest embroidery design has been copied to your device.

4 Select the option Send To and another window appears. Scroll down to the memory stick drive—Disgo (E:)—at the bottom of the list, and click on it. This sends the embroidery design to your hardware. The original embroidery design remains in your Embroidery Designs folder, while the copied replica is on your USB memory stick. Minimize this window as before. You now have two minimized windows.

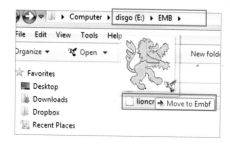

6 If your embroidery machine does not require you to drag the embroidery design into a folder, as it is unformatted, you have now completed the move. If you do need to drag the design in, highlight the design by left clicking on it and holding your finger down. Drag the embroidery design into the folder. Then open the folder and drag the embroidery design into one of the subfolders. Click on the red cross in the top right-hand corner to close Drive (E:).

device and ready to go or in Documents and need to be dragged into the Embroidery Designs folder.

Some embroidery design CD-ROMs have multi-format design sets. In this case, the opened design list will include folders with the format as the folder name. You must send the whole folder to its destination instead of a single file.

BACK UP YOUR DESIGNS

Buy two smaller-capacity USB memory sticks rather than one large one, and back up all of your embroidery designs to the second one. The capacity of these external drives is huge. The embroidery machine needs to load all of the designs on your stick before you can select the one you want to stitch out. If you have too many on your stick, this can take a while. Keep only a few at a time on the hardware you are using daily, and the rest on your computer and the backup USB stick.

DIRECT CABLE LINK FROM MACHINE TO COMPUTER

Some machines have a direct cable link. The sewing machine becomes the external drive. One end of the USB cable that came with the machine's accessories goes into a small USB port on the machine and the other end goes into a USB port on your computer. The drivers in your computer are automatically updated when you first make the cable link.

When linked, embroidery machines usually come up in Drive (F:). However, the machine may appear in another drive, depending on your computer. You then need to open the communication between the two, using an icon on the machine that opens the PC Link. Once this is open you can send embroidery designs to the drive your embroidery machine opens, using the same method as sending to a USB memory stick.

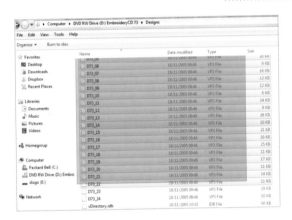

◀ Multiple files have been highlighted here and can be moved in one batch.

READING FILES ON EXTERNAL DRIVES AND CDS

In order to use a design purchased on a CD-ROM, you need to copy the design from the CD to your external device or onto your computer, unless you have an external CD-ROM drive that works with your embroidery machine. Always make sure your design CD contains a format suitable for your embroidery machine.

In this demonstration, Embroidery CD #73 Husqvarna Viking Blooming Elegance is being opened. A Husqvana Viking Ruby machine that can read .VP3 format is being used. There will also be times when you want to see what is stored on your external drive, using the method described here: this could be when you want to organize or delete files and folders.

Insert your device or your CD. A window appears. At the top of the window, the Drive you are opening appears. This could say Drive (D:), which is your DVD RW drive; Drive (E:), which is usually a memory stick or flash card; Drive (F:), which may be your sewing machine; and so on. The letter in brackets beside the Drive ( ) tells you what you are looking at. Here a CD is put into the DVD RW drive with embroidery designs on; therefore Drive (D:) is opening. The window says AutoPlay. Click on the yellow folder icon that says Open Folder to View Files.

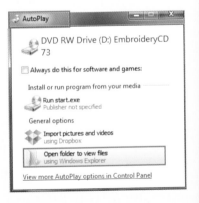

Once an embroidery design has been put into the PC Link folder in your embroidery machine, you can sew it out. Some machines require that you save the design into the machine's memory before sewing; others don't.

DELETING FILES

To delete a file, whether in the Embroidery Designs folder, on a USB memory stick or flash card, or on the embroidery machine, left click on the file or folder, scroll down to Delete, and right click. The file will go to the Recycle bin and be deleted.

SAFELY REMOVING HARDWARE

You must safely remove your USB memory stick or flash card to minimize the likelihood of it failing and losing your data. Never just pull it out of the computer.

1 Go to the task bar at the bottom right-hand corner of the screen and find an icon that shows Safely Remove Hardware and Eject Media when your mouse hovers over it. It is usually a small USB stick image with a green checkmark on it.

2 Right click on the icon for a list of options. Scroll down to the manufacturer name or drive letter name of your hardware and click on it once. You will now be told it is safe to remove your device.

3 Your external device is now ready to be removed from the computer and put into the embroidery machine.

4 Take it to the machine and put it into the correct slot. When opened, the folder will have your embroidery designs in.

SENDING IS DUPLICATING

Sending does not mean removing. It means that you are making a copy. The original remains where it is and a copy is made in the new destination.

ORGANIZING YOUR EXTERNAL DRIVE

You can organize your embroidery files on a memory stick or flash card in the same way as folders and subfolders in Documents on the computer (see page 28).

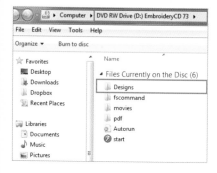

2 You will see all the folders and files that are on the CD or device. In the top toolbar you will see the details of the drive opened. In this example it is DVD RW Drive (D:) and EmbroideryCD 73. There are six items on the CD. Double click on the file labeled Designs to open it.

3 The full set of embroidery designs contained in the collection appears as a list.

4 Right click on the design of your choice. Software on this computer shows the full detail of the embroidery design: if you don't have this software, your right click may not show as much information. Go down the second list and select Send To. Then, in the second small window that appears, select either Documents or your external device drive, depending on where you want to put the embroidery design.

5 Once the embroidery design is sent to its destination, you can close the CD by clicking on the top right-hand red cross.

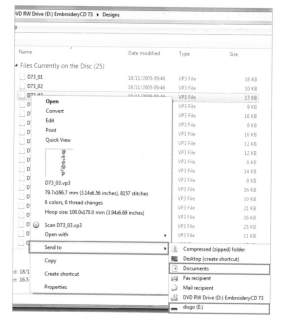

Embroidery software

Embroidery software for your computer, used in conjunction with your embroidery machine, can help you organize your embroidery designs and allow you to create your own designs.

CONSIDER YOUR DECISION

Before choosing your software, think about what you want to achieve now and how much more you will want to do in the future. Do you simply want to organize purchased designs? Do you want to make minor adjustments to an existing design? Will you one day want to create your own designs?

Turning clip art into stitches can be done using a customizing software package, but turning your own artwork into an embroidery design, then going back and altering the stitches, takes much more expertise and can only be achieved with full digitizing software. Customizing software is around a third of the price of digitizing software. A mid-range software, with all the editing and customizing capabilities plus some basic digitizing, may be the one you want. On the other hand, if you want to create your own designs and use features such as cross stitch, expect to pay at least $1,200 for a full digitizing suite. Then there are necessary upgrades to software to keep up with the ever-changing computer, which will add to your costs. Eventually, if you don't keep up with the upgrades, your software becomes obsolete.

SOFTWARE PACKAGES

A full-suite software package will include everything you need; alternatively, you can buy individual modules as and when you need them or buy the customizing and editing package alone. Upgrades to boxed software are available through the company website as a download, or can be bought on a CD-ROM.

Select multi-format software where possible, since this can read and save designs in different formats, which means that you can buy a design in a different format than your machine uses, open the design using the software, and re-save it in your format. Multi-format software is very useful, and most software packages available today are multi-format, but do check before you buy.

In a box

Most people prefer to have something in their hand when purchasing software, and buying it in the box is the usual route. The box will usually include a user manual, a CD-ROM, and a dongle—a security device that fits into a USB port. If a dongle is required, the software won't work properly without it.

Computer based

With computer-based software you won't actually own a box, but will have a unique registration number or pass code that you key in on installation of the software once it has downloaded. The numbers or codes are entered when you install the software on any computer, so don't worry when it comes time to upgrade to a new computer: you will be able to re-install the software as long as you have this information. You are usually limited, however, by the number of computers the software can be installed on at any given time.

COMPUTER OPERATING SYSTEMS

Most software is designed for use with Windows, although some companies are now making their software compatible with Mac operating systems. The operating systems that any software will work on will be listed on the box or download information, so always check for compatibility with your own computer before you buy.

TABLETS

Apps for these devices have just begun to be available. These are ideal for those on the go, who can use the apps to create or alter embroidery designs. Apps are also available for sorting out colors, customizing designs, and limited designing of your own.

ORGANIZING SOFTWARE

Organization software is a useful addition if you purchase customizing software rather than the full suite of digitizing software. This software lets you display your embroidery designs as images on your computer. If you purchase a full digitizing suite, then you won't need this extra package.

CUSTOMIZING SOFTWARE

Editing or customizing software is the smaller package, thus it is a lot less expensive than digitizing software. This software lets you extensively edit an existing design, allowing you to alter the original by changing colors and sizes, adding lettering, and combining designs within a hoop area for perfect layout. Available tasks include rotating with precision, mirror-imaging horizontally and vertically, and merging other embroidery designs, all of which can be difficult to do on an embroidery machine's sewing screen. Customizing software lets you see the design in realistic preview, and some packages will allow you to redraw the embroidery in slow motion so that you can see how it will stitch out.

Many packages include an autodigitizing feature and will allow you to go back to the created embroidery design to make minor adjustments. Some allow you to create your own designs using scanned images or with freehand drawing tools. You can also print templates of any creation or design for easy positioning.

The much smaller customizing packages are suitable for those who want to make a few changes but are not interested in creating their own embroidery designs.

DIGITIZING SOFTWARE

Digitizing software is the complete package. It allows you to make many changes to an existing design—for example, removing sections you don't want, changing the stitching order, merging designs and color sorting, removing overlapping segments, laying out into a large design, splitting a design for smaller hoops, and much more.

Digitizing software will have a powerful built-in graphics program, with which you can create your own embroideries from scanned images, including your own sketches or drawings, or you can start from scratch using freehand drawing tools.

Digitizing packages contain an enormous number of stitches, from embossed fill stitches to different run stitches. You are able to break down your embroidery designs into "objects" and change stitch direction, remove/add stitches, alter the running order, and much more. This software lets you decide on stitch size and direction, select the underlay (the stitch structure upon which an embroidery design is built), and even select the fabric you want to stitch on—called pull compensation because the software decides how much stretch or give the fabric will have and compensates for this accordingly. Other features include appliqué, photo-stitch, and cross-stitch tools.

Most full digitizing packages include a huge amount of embroidery designs for you to use, as well as a large selection of fonts that automatically load onto your computer when the software is installed.

If you want to design and create individual and unique embroideries, then a full suite is the way forward. Digitizing properly is a highly skilled task that takes patience to learn. You have to be prepared to put the time and effort in, since there is no quick way to master digitizing your own designs.

▲ There is a huge variety of fonts available for all your monogramming needs.

SPECIFIC SOFTWARE

There are a number of software packages that concentrate on single disciplines—for example, software for lettering and monogramming alone, or quilting software for creating your own quilting designs and laying out a full quilt. Explore the options and possibilities to make sure that you don't repeat your purchases—for example, quilting software may already be included in a full suite of software from a different company.

YOU DON'T NEED UNZIPPING SOFTWARE

Many people new to unzipping compressed folders on their computer buy an unzipping program. This is not necessary; instead, simply unzip using the built-in program in Windows (see page 33).

COMPUTER-BASED SOFTWARE REGISTRATION

Registration numbers are usually delivered by email. It is important to keep a record of these, plus any emails relating to your transaction. Whenever you receive email notification of registration numbers or pass codes, copy and paste the whole email into a Word document, in case you change your email address or lose your password in the future.

A software overview

The software programs detailed over the next few pages are by no means the only options, but give an idea of what is available. The features listed represent an overview only, so collect brochures to find out what is included in the various packages, and compare them all before making a decision.

You don't have to buy software that is the same brand as your machine, providing it can save to your embroidery machine's format. It is a good idea to download free trial versions of software where possible, or visit your dealer and ask to try out different ones.

SOFTWARE PACKAGES
These can be a complete suite, the smaller customizing versions, or stand-alone technique software.

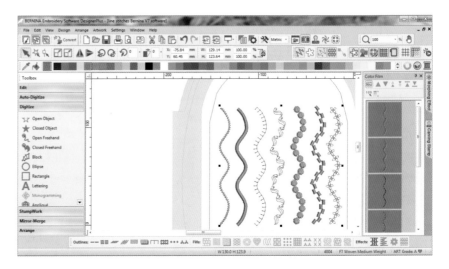

Bernina Embroidery Software 7 DesignerPlus is the full suite in one package. It includes a powerful graphics program from Corel, so all your own artwork can be prepared within the program before digitizing. Facilities for needle punching, trapunto, and three-dimensional embroidery creation give a wide variety of creative possibilities. The program includes automatic digitizing as well as manual hand drawing on screen to create objects that can be filled with a huge variety of stitches, including embossed fills, fancy fills, and carved effects. The creations can be fine-tuned on screen and previewed realistically on a diverse selection of articles before being saved to a wide variety of formats. A full monogramming program is included that allows you to create monograms and fancy lettering, add borders, line stitches (see above), decorative stitches, and more. The

quilting program is excellent and includes powerful tools to create impressive quilts, including creating your own quilting embroidery designs.

Bernina Embroidery Software 7 EditorPlus is a very good mid-range software for the beginner. It has all the usual customizing features and lets you create your own designs by scanning images or using freehand drawing tools included in the CorelDRAW graphics program. It includes a wide range of stitch patterns and fill stitches, embossed fills, and runs to edit your creations, and lets you preview your designs in realistic settings. The software includes a quilting program that lets you create your own quilting designs and plan the layout of your quilt.

▲ Each digitizing software program has many different embroidery line stitches. The line stitches may include (as shown here) stem, satin, blanket, pattern, candlewicking, and blackwork. Many of the stitches mimic hand embroidery stitches. You can adjust the thickness of the stitched line, as well as the spacing between individual motifs, to create the exact line you want.

BROTHER SOFTWARE

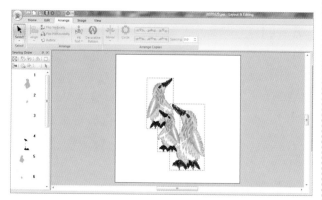

▲ Small embroidery designs may be combined to create either a border or a larger design. Within digitizing software programs, there is the ability to resize a design, rotate it, or mirror image it. The left side of the screen shows the stitching order of the objects within the embroidery design combination.

Brother PE Design Next is the full digitizing package and includes auto-punch tools, auto-appliqué tools, and photo-stitch, cross-stitch, and special lettering programs. You can create designs quickly from scanned photographs, images, or drawings, and manually edit and fine-tune them afterward. The freehand drawing tool allows you to draw your own motifs. The program includes many fills, fancy stitches, decorative runs, and extras such as candlewicking. You can also create embroidery designs from decorative stitches similar to those on your sewing machine. The business tools make this the ideal software for those who want semi-industrial capabilities.

Brother PE Design Plus is the smaller package for those who want editing or customizing facilities with a step toward creating their own designs. The program allows you to make edits to previously digitized designs and make changes including rotating, mirror-imaging, and placement (see above) within the user-defined hoops. Brother PE Design Plus also has a number of built-in designs and fonts from which you can create customized motifs. The program includes automatic appliqué and photo-stitch tools, and allows the user to turn photos and scanned designs or clip art into embroidery.

JANOME SOFTWARE

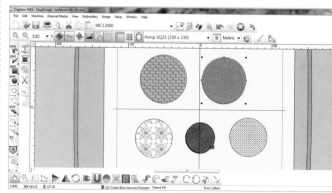

▲ Digitizing embroidery software has a wide range of fill stitches available. They include fills that give a solid effect (for instance) a weave fill, and other fills that give a more open look. The designer can also change the size of any embroidery object to the exact size that is required and has a choice of many colors.

Digitizer MBX V4.5 is the full suite in one package. It includes the CorelDRAW X5 Essentials graphics program, which makes the preparation of scanned images, drawings, and photographs before digitizing easier. Click to Stitch creates embroidery instantly, and you have the ability to fine-tune the design afterward in Easy Edit.

Freehand drawing tools allow you to create your own embroideries, and you can then select from a large variety of fill and run stitches to further enhance your creation. The advanced freehand tools provide a different method of creating shapes and lines that is more natural than the traditional digitizing methods already used in Digitizer.

When used in conjunction with a tablet and pen, creating embroidery is as natural as drawing with a pencil and paper. Appliqué, hand-look, candlewicking, and sculpture stitches are available within the program. Monogramming and advanced shaping and lettering tools are also included, together with 100 fonts. The Easy Edit screen allows you to make changes, alter designs, and arrange in hoops before saving to most home formats.

Janome Digitizer Jr is the baby brother to the full suite. The software can import designs, resize, make edits to existing designs, and create monograms and lettering using 16 built-in fonts. There is a selection of decorative fill stitches (see above) and run stitches for design editing. The software writes to limited formats for other machines.

MODULAR PACKAGES

These can be purchased as one package if you want the full suite, or as modules that can be added to a basic package as and when you want them.

Husqvarna Viking or Pfaff 6D Professional Embroidery System can be a complete digitizing system with everything included, or purchased in software modules. 6D Embroidery lets you edit and customize designs, create lettering, and make changes, whereas 6D Embroidery Extra has many more features, including 6D Wizards to autodigitize with the ExpressDesign Wizard, Quiltblock Wizard, or Photostitch Wizard, which you can go back to and fine-tune later.

Other modules include 6D Stitch Editor, which allows you to go back over your embroideries and reshape, restyle, and make improvements; 6D Card Shop, which has templates for over 600 embroidered greetings card ideas; 6D Photostitch, to turn your photographs and images into stitch; 6D Cross Stitcher, to design your own cross stitch; 6D Family Tree to make unique creations using your own family history; 6D Design Creator to create your own perfect design with unlimited possibilities, including the gradient fills shown in the objects above; 6D Font Digitizing to turn TrueType fonts into lettering and save them as your own alphabets, as well as a huge selection already in the software; and 6D Sketch, which

▲ The direction of the gradient may also be selected. This offers unlimited possibilities for the shading of embroidery to create a more dramatic look.

allows you to freehand draw and save the drawing as an embroidery file. The package mixes and matches, so you only buy the elements you need.

TruEmbroidery is a complete modular system for Macintosh computers. It is compatible with most home embroidery machines and consists of three modules and two assistants. The modules are TruE Studio, TruE Modify, and TruE Create. The assistants are TruE QuickCreate Assistant and TruE Portrait Assistant.

In TruE Studio you can adjust, personalize, and combine embroidery designs, including rotate, mirror-image, reflect, and save with stitch density control. The program has over 1,200 embroidery designs and 100 fonts. In TruE Modify you can alter a design by selecting fills and stitches to modify and improve the stitch-out quality with features such as stitch compensation. In TruE Create you can design your own motifs using freehand tools, or create automatically with the QuickCreate feature. The program has features for digitizing your own lace with lace tools and a choice of thousands of stitch effects. QuickCreate Assistant allows you to create embroideries from clip art and Portrait Assistant turns photographs into realistic embroidered portraits.

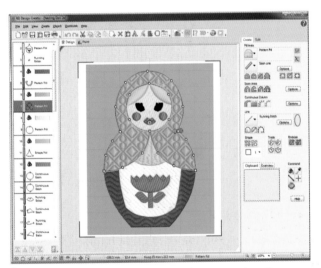

▲ Objects do not have to be a solid color. In each software program there is the possibility to create a gradient fill, which may consist of just two colors or, in some softwares, multiple colored gradients.

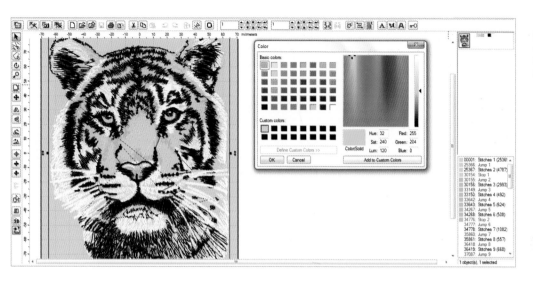

◀ Using software, it is possible to change the colors that appear in a design.

COMPUTER-BASED EMBROIDERY SOFTWARE

Embird is a computer-based software with a password and registration number. The basic software allows you to edit, customize, alter colors, merge designs, split designs, rotate, mirror-image horizontally and vertically, and alter design size with density altered automatically. There is a freehand select mode, points editing mode, and zoom mode. You can alter colors, delete selections of a design, and duplicate with ease. There is a stitch preview, a sew simulator, and a slow redraw to see how your embroidery design stitches out on the screen. It is multi-format, allowing you to write to a large selection of formats.

Optional extras purchased as plug-ins include Studio for digitizing your own designs; Iconizer for viewing your embroidery designs; Cross Stitch to design your own cross-stitch embroideries; Sfumato, which is the same as photo stitch, to create photo-realistic portraits; and Font Engine to turn fonts into your own alphabets.

▶ The digital image of the tiger (right) was drawn using Adobe Photoshop by Daniel Loveday. He added contours and shadows to create an image with depth and definition that would translate well when stitched out. After using digitizing software, the image was stitched out on 100 percent cotton with a heavy woven cutaway stabilizer to support the density of the design.

CHAPTER 2

Tools and materials

Lovely machine embroidery depends on a number of factors coming together: your choice of embroidery design and its density, the needles you use, the thread you select, the fabric you want to use, and finally, the correct stabilizer for all of the above. Once you have made these important decisions, you need to learn how to place your embroidery designs where you want them, how to line several up to make a larger display, and how to hoop and embroider difficult fabrics. All of this key material is covered in this helpful section.

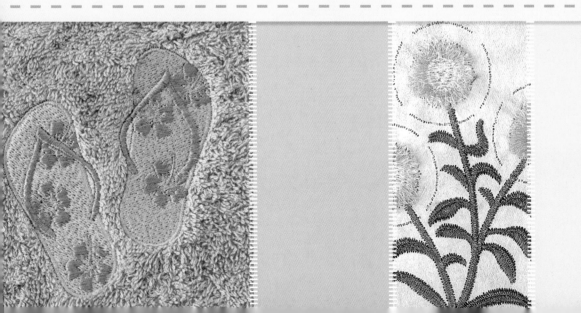

▲ Low-density design
Stitch count: 4,588
Size: 3 x 2¹/₆₄in (77.8 x 75.2mm)
The stitches in the center of the heart are triple run stitches and there are no solid fill areas. A medium-weight tearaway stabilizer was used.

▲ High-density design
Stitch count: 7,755
Size: 3¹/₃ x 3¹/₁₀in (84.8 x 79.8mm)
The stitching for this heart is heavy fill without gaps and so it is classed as a dense embroidery design. It has been stitched out on cutaway stabilizer.

All about stabilizers

Stabilizers support the stitches in a machine embroidery design. A machine will not embroider a fabric hooped by itself without some kind of stabilizer underneath. It is the stabilizer that supports and holds the stitching, not the fabric—and the higher your design density, the stronger the stabilizer required.

DESIGN DENSITY EXPLAINED

An embroidery design has many stitches. The "design density" is the number of stitches per square inch of a hoop embroidery area is known as the design density. A design that fits into a hoop embroidery area of 4 x 4in (10 x 10cm) with 9,000 stitches is going to be much denser than the same 9,000 stitches in a hoop with an embroidery area of 6 x 10in (15 x 25cm). High-density designs tend to be more solid than low-density designs. A cartoon character that is completely full of stitches would be classed as high density, whereas an embroidery of an open, stylized flower with unstitched areas would be classed as low density. High-density embroidery requires a better stabilizer than low-density embroidery, regardless of the fabric used.

The number of stitches in a design is always stipulated, whether printed on a sheet, in a booklet, or on the machine screen when it is loaded. Look at the embroidery properly. Is it open? Is it solid? How many stitches are there for the hoop embroidery area you are using? Is the embroidery design high density, low density, or somewhere in the middle? Once you know how dense the design is, it is time to select a stabilizer.

If the wrong stabilizer is used, all sorts of problems occur: stitches are misaligned; outlines that should touch the main embroidery have gaps; the embroidery puckers up around the edges when removed from the hoop. If any of these happen, it is most likely to be down to the choice of stabilizer.

Unfortunately, choosing a stabilizer is not an exact science, so a certain amount of trial and error is required. Always do a test before embarking on the real thing. If it doesn't work out exactly as it should, try again with a different stabilizer backing.

STABILIZER STOCK

A basic stock of a few different types of stabilizer will cover most needs. You can build a stash slowly, then make replacements as your stock dwindles. A good recommended basic stock of stabilizers for new embroidery machine owners would include:

• Selection of tearaway weights, light, medium, and strong
• Good-quality sticky-backed tearaway
• Good iron-on fusible tearaway
• Good-quality medium cutaway
• Good-quality polymesh cutaway
• Good-quality iron-on fusible polymesh cutaway
• Water-soluble fabric
• Thin water-soluble film
• Good-quality water-soluble sticky-backed stabilizer

TEARAWAY STABILIZERS

Tearaway stabilizers can be gently torn away from the reverse of the work once the embroidery is complete. Work from the edges of the design to prevent stitches from pulling.

Basic tearaway

Tearaway stabilizer is essential to a machine embroiderer's kit, and makes a good stabilizer for most woven fabrics. It is made from a nonwoven material that tears easily when ripped, but is strong enough to support stitches, and is available in black or white. The basic tearaway is hooped with the fabric (see Hooping method 1, page 62).

The basic tearaway is only strong enough to support light to medium stitch counts. If your design isn't stitching properly, then the tearaway stabilizer you are using isn't strong enough. For example, if the stabilizer has ripped apart while sewing on the underneath, the stitches are offline, and the fabric puckers as you embroider, you need to try the next weight up, or swap to a cutaway stabilizer.

Sticky-backed tearaway

This stabilizer has an adhesive coating covered by a protective layer. The stabilizer is hooped by itself, with the protective layer facing up. The protective layer is then removed to reveal the adhesive coating, onto which you gently lay your fabric (see Hooping method 2, page 64). Hooping in this way means you don't have to worry about the fabric being too tight or off grain, because you don't actually hoop the fabric at all. This stabilizer also has the advantage of being able to hold still those fabrics that have a slight stretch.

▲ This redwork line design required a basic medium-weight tearaway stabilizer.

Sticky-backed tearaway stabilizer is generally recommended for hard-to-hoop items such as collars, socks, ribbons, etc. However, it is a good all-round stabilizer since the tearaway backing is strong and many people find the hooping method easier than the alternative method of putting the top hoop, fabric, and stabilizer into the bottom hoop.

Iron-on fusible tearaway

Iron-on tearaway stabilizer has an adhesive coating that is released when heated. It is used to hold fabric still while embroidering. It is quite thin and so can be used in conjunction with another stabilizer should it be needed. A pressing motion, rather than actual ironing, makes the stabilizer smooth and releases the glue more evenly. The stabilizer and fabric are then hooped together (see Hooping method 1, page 62). The embroidery is completed and the excess stabilizer is lifted from the back and torn away. Iron-on tearaway

stabilizers will only work for the same stitch counts as nonfusible tearaways. The same theory applies. If the stabilizer is beginning to break up, or your embroidery shifts, you need to move on to a cutaway stabilizer.

Water-activated sticky-backed tearaway

This is a much stronger, stickier tearaway stabilizer. The stabilizer is hooped and then the surface, which has a silicone-based adhesive that reacts with water, is lightly sprayed with water or moistened with a damp cloth. The glue is activated and begins to stick. It is a very strong stick indeed and will hold a heavy fabric stable. To remove the fabric after embroidery, the glue needs to be reactivated with water and the fabric pulled carefully away. This stabilizer remains firm in the finished embroidery so select it only when you don't need your embroidery to be very soft.

▼ This dense design required two stabilizers to support the stitches.

AVOID LAYING LOOSE STABILIZER UNDER THE HOOP

It is not a good idea to add further layers of stabilizer under the hoop if one layer of tearaway isn't enough. If a tearaway stabilizer breaks down, it is because it isn't strong enough. Adding further layers only causes the embroidery design to become stiffer. Swap the stabilizer to a stronger tearaway or a cutaway stabilizer.

CUTAWAY STABILIZERS

Cutaway stabilizers are very strong and can support an enormous number of stitches. A cutaway stabilizer will remain in place and doesn't disintegrate over time. You need scissors to trim away the excess from the back after embroidery: if you attempt to pull it away, you will pull the stitches out.

Cutaway stabilizers really are a good investment. If you are planning a heavy stitch count, or embroidery with heavy fill areas, then cutaway stabilizer should be used. It eliminates many of the problems found when using tearaway stabilizer.

Woven synthetic cutaway

Cutaway stabilizers are made from white, durable, synthetic fiber. They also come in different weights, so do a test to see whether you need a light, medium, or strong one. Usually, a medium one will be sufficient.

Polymesh cutaway

The very new nylon mesh varieties of cutaway are super to use. They are made of sheer nylon, very light but very strong. They can be called polymesh, sheer, or no-show mesh. Once sewn, the mesh can hardly be seen. It is especially good where the remaining edges of stabilizer around a design may be seen as a shadow from the right side. They are very versatile because they are suitable for nearly all fabrics. They are available in off-white, natural beige, and black.

Iron-on fusible polymesh cutaway

The mesh cutaway stabilizers also come in an iron-on version. These can be ironed onto stretch or knit fabrics before hooping.

Water-activated sticky-backed cutaway

If you want a very strong sticky cutaway, then look at a water-activated version. It can be hooped on its own and the stick activated with a water spray or damp cloth. Water is also needed to remove the excess stabilizer before trimming. Try not to get these products too wet—damp is sufficient.

This product is great for supporting stitches. It is recommended for harder-to-hoop fabric, such as velvet, and hard-to-hoop areas such as collars and cuffs. Nevertheless, it is a good all-rounder and can be used in much the same way as sticky-backed tearaway stabilizer, especially if you prefer not to hoop your fabric.

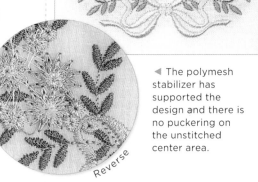

◀ The polymesh stabilizer has supported the design and there is no puckering on the unstitched center area.

WATER-SOLUBLE STABILIZERS

These are also called washaways or solvies. The stabilizer is hooped by itself and the embroidery is stitched directly onto the stabilizer. The stabilizer is completely dissolved with water once the embroidery has been completed. Water-soluble stabilizer is used for freestanding lace, as a topping to stop stitches sinking into

BRANDING

Trade names are a source of great confusion. The stabilizers listed here are manufactured by different companies and sold under their own names.

The secret is to find a brand you like or can buy easily from your own dealer, then continue to purchase from that range. If you come across one that isn't available from your selected range, then look for another brand—but do be careful to read exactly what it is and what it can do.

▼ This fringe design has been stitched with cutaway stabilizer. The stabilizer has remained totally secure, with no broken areas on the underside.

deep-pile fabrics, and for ornate three-dimensional work. It can be used for cutwork, reverse cutwork embroidering on fine net and mesh, and heirloom sewing—in fact, anywhere you don't want a stabilizer to remain in the fabric or project after embroidery. It goes without saying that your fabric must be washable!

Each water-soluble stabilizer is slightly different in appearance and weight. They also need different water temperatures to dissolve, from cold water to tepid to hot. If you don't follow the instructions, the stabilizer will not disperse correctly.

Ultra water-soluble stabilizer

The ultra heavyweight water-soluble stabilizers will obviously hold a higher stitch count than the lighter films. They are rather like a thick clear plastic to look at and feel. There are a few brands to choose from, so test them out, see which you prefer, and keep at least one or two in your stash. These tear if the needle is too big or slightly worn, so always use a new needle.

Water-soluble fabric

Water-soluble fabric is also known as washable fabric, solufleece, or even soluble fabric. It is easy to use, but also easy to distort when hooping. You hoop it as if it is fabric, straight and even with the grain. It is tempting to tug at it to make it taut in the hoop, but this will distort the fibers, and when it has dissolved the embroidery could be

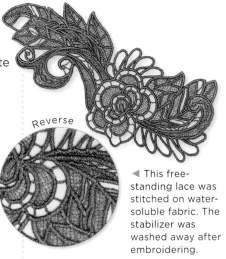

Reverse

◀ This free-standing lace was stitched on water-soluble fabric. The stabilizer was washed away after embroidering.

misshapen. Always use two layers hooped together, since the stitch penetration will rip one layer alone.

Water-soluble sticky-backed stabilizer

This water-soluble stabilizer has a sticky coating and protective top paper layer and is hooped on its own. The protective layer is removed with a pin to reveal the sticky coating. The fabric is laid over the exposed sticky surface. After embroidery the fabric is washed and the stabilizer washes away, leaving only the fabric and embroidery behind. This is a must for embroidering on light fabrics and washable sheers, such as polyester georgette. It is quite expensive to purchase, so only use it when you have no alternative.

Water-soluble film

This is a thin, washable film that is only strong enough to use as a topping for deep-pile fabrics. The film is put onto the fabric after hooping and prevents the stitches from sinking into the pile. Do not try to use this in any other way, since it is not strong enough.

HEATAWAY STABILIZERS

Heataway stabilizers are usually used where a fabric isn't washable but must be able to withstand a very high temperature. The iron heats the stabilizer that, in theory, disintegrates, leaving brownish flakes that can be brushed away. The iron must be very hot, otherwise you can end up with a gluey mess. Each manufacturer suggests a different temperature, so read the packaging. Steam must not come into contact with this stabilizer, because it makes a sticky mess.

Using baking parchment over and below your embroidery prevents the stabilizer from sticking to your ironing board and your iron. If you can find the right blend of temperature, fabric, and baking parchment to make the stabilizer disintegrate properly, then you have a winning combination.

Heataway film

This is a bobbly, plastic film that can support many stitches. The embroidery is completed and the excess stabilizer is removed with a hot iron. It is also brilliant for making badges or freestanding items that need to have body in them. The embroidery itself needs to be completely solid with no gaps. When the embroidery is finished, cut the finished piece away from the stabilizer. You are left with a clean edge.

Heataway fabric

This looks similar to linen and is hooped with the fabric. The embroidery is completed and the excess cut away as much as possible. The final pieces are removed with a hot iron. It is only suitable for low to medium stitch counts, because it isn't as stable as heataway film.

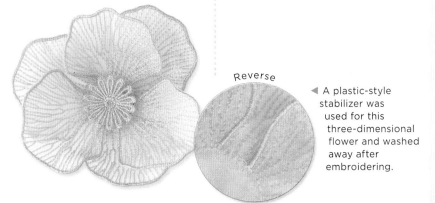

Reverse

◀ A plastic-style stabilizer was used for this three-dimensional flower and washed away after embroidering.

Needle know-how

The right needle makes all the difference to your embroidery. Match needle to fabric correctly and your stitches will be smooth and well defined, without any holes punched around the design.

Insert your needle into the machine with the flat side backward. Push the needle up as far as it will go and tighten the screw. Machine embroidery is fast and a loose needle will cause problems.

TYPES OF NEEDLE
Machine embroidery needles are designed for machine embroidery so should always be used, unless a specialty needle is required (see below). A machine embroidery needle has a longer, deeper scarf where the thread sits than a machine sewing needle. This is to allow for the high speed of the threads running through the needle. The eye is also larger and rounder, so the thread causes less friction when passing through.

NEEDLE SIZES
Needle selection is based on fabric. You need to use the correct size because the amount of needle penetration in and around a design causes holes in the fabric, which are unsightly if they are too big. The needles range from size 60 for extremely fine fabric through to size 110 for upholstery fabrics.

SPECIALTY NEEDLES
Occasionally, an embroidery design calls for a specialty needle. These needles are a little more expensive than ordinary needles but, as they are seldom used, they do last a long time.

Twin needles
These are needles with two points, with a determined space

between the points ranging from $1/16$ to $3/16$in (2 to 5mm). These needles require two threads, one threaded normally, the other either on a bobbin or another spool of thread on your top spool pin (this can be built-in or an accessory) and threaded alongside the first but through the eye of the second needle. An embroidery design that uses a twin needle will be digitized to allow for the specified size of twin needle. Always use the needle size stated in the design, otherwise you will hit the needle plate and break it. The design's documentation will tell you when to use the twin needle.

Wing needles
These needles have a flare on each side to push the fabric out

Twin needle: The embroidery is stitched on cotton fabric with a lightweight cutaway stabilizer, and so a size 80 embroidery needle was used. A size 80 twin needle with a $3/32$in (2.5mm) gap was used in the twin needle areas.

Wing needle: The embroidery design is stitched on cotton fabric with a lightweight cutaway stabilizer, so a size 80 embroidery needle was used. The wing needle area was sewn with a size 100 wing needle.

Embroidery needle size 90: This needle was chosen in order to penetrate the dense denim fabric. Denim can support higher stitch counts without needing a heavy stabilizer. An iron-on fusible tearaway was used to hold the stretch in the denim still.

of the way, thus creating a hole. They are best used on natural fibers. An embroidery design that uses a wing needle will tell you in its documentation which part of the design requires the wing needle and which size to use. Part of the finished embroidery design will have decorative holes resembling heirloom sewing. Never resize a wing needle design; the wing needle sections are digitized at exactly the right size.

Topstitch needles

These are used if the thread is thicker than normal—for example, decorative or wool-based threads. The point is larger, but so is the needle eye. They are available in different sizes but a size 90 is suitable for most machine-embroidery requirements. Use the topstitch needle for the part of the design that uses the thicker thread and swap back to an embroidery needle afterward.

Metallic needles

These are used with metallic threads: the thread will break and snap if you don't use one. The groove is deep for the thread to sit in and the eye is large and more oblong than round. Metallic needles range in size and you select the size according to your fabric. Sizes 75, 80, and 90 should be sufficient for most applications.

Ballpoint needles

These are not generally used in machine embroidery, but can be useful when stitching on stretch or T-shirt fabric. The point is rounded, so it slips between the fibers rather than splitting them. Unfortunately, they don't have the design of machine embroidery needles so you are likely to experience thread shredding and breaking. Whether or not you use these really depends on the quality of the T-shirt or stretch fabric.

NEEDLE BREAKAGES

Needles break a lot and this is probably not because you are doing something wrong. A needle breaks when the machine wants to stop suddenly. It is the machine's way of saying that it wants to stop sewing. Have a look to see what the problem is before continuing. Most likely is that your top thread has twisted and jammed, the bobbin thread has caught up, or the part of the embroidery you are sewing is too thick. Rectify the problem, switch to a new needle, and continue sewing. If the embroidery is too dense for the size you are using, go up a size and try again.

NEEDLE LIFE SPAN

Needles do not last long. The life span of a new needle is roughly 10,000 stitches before it begins to blunt. A blunt needle will cause problems: threads will break, pull the embroidery out into loops, catch on stitches, and generally spoil your work. Change needles often. A blunt needle is the cause of most embroidery problems.

Metallic needle: This design is stitched on cotton with a medium-weight cutaway stabilizer and an size 80 embroidery needle. The metallic areas were stitched with a size 80 metallic needle.

Ballpoint needle: Stretch T-shirt fabric is used here. A size 70 ballpoint needle was used to stop the fibers in the fabric from splitting. To hold the stretch on the fabric still, fusible polymesh stabilizer was used.

Choosing machine embroidery threads

Machine embroidery threads are manufactured for the purpose. They are softer to the touch than sewing threads, much smoother, and have the ability to spread as they lay on the fabric, thus covering a larger area.

Having paid a large amount of money for your machine, it is sensible to use good-quality thread: the results are far superior, without thread breakages, tension problems, and the general headaches that go alongside cheap, poorly manufactured thread. A spool cap must always be used to hold reels in place.

TYPES OF THREAD

The brand or type of thread you choose for your main collection is down to personal choice. At first you may feel embroidery threads are more expensive than sewing threads, but this is not the case. Purchasing the threads in 1,100-yard (1,000-m) spools feels extravagant, but 220-yard (200-m) spools do not go very far, so it is more economical to select fewer colors in larger spools than more colors in small amounts. Try to select one brand to begin with and build on that collection. Eventually you will have collected all the colors and only need to replace those that run out. It is a good idea to buy a thread chart from the manufacturer, which will have the threads wound onto a strong piece of card with the thread numbers next to them. When you get going, you can introduce new brands to your collection.

Threads for machine embroidery generally fall into two categories—natural and synthetic. The most popular choice for this type of embroidery is synthetic, which can withstand the high sewing speeds with fewer breakages.

Natural fibers

Cotton thread is expensive, but is soft, spreads well, and gives a lovely matte finish. It is generally used with specific embroidery designs to give an authentic look—for example, computerized machine cross stitch. The color range is limited when compared to synthetic threads. Cotton thread is available in different weights, although most are restricted to 220-yard (200-m) spools, so building a cotton collection is expensive. It is best saved for specific purposes.

Silk is a beautiful, lustrous thread, but it is very expensive. It doesn't withstand high speeds very well and is very restricted in colors available.

Wool threads have recently become available for specialty embroidery designs. Wool is used for imitation crewelwork, where the thread has to be thicker. It is also used in wool designs where animal fur is predominant: once embroidered, the wool is brushed to resemble fur.

▲ Wool thread is used to add texture.

▲ Cotton thread gives a lovely matte finish.

Synthetic fibers

Rayon is an alternative to silk thread and displays the same qualities, but with the bonus of being very suitable for machine embroidery. It has a subtle sheen and is available in different weights and in a huge range of colors.

▲ Rayon thread is excellent for sewing at high speeds.

It glides through the needle easily and, because it is synthetic, it is very strong and will produce great results at the high speeds required.

Polyester is the most widely used thread for machine embroidery. Like other synthetics, it is manufactured with a waxy coating to help it slip through the needle easily. It is available in a huge variety of colors and is colorfast to 200°F (95°C). It is also the best value for money and is available on spools of up to 5,500 yards (5,000m). Polyester produces the highest sheen and the finish is very attractive. The thread is very strong, so there are fewer breakages. The high sheen remains in the embroidery wash after wash, so polyester is a good all-round performer.

Bobbinfil

Bobbinfil is very fine, 60-weight polyester thread. As embroidery stitches, an underneath stitch is made. The finer the bobbinfil, the less dense the underneath threads. Most embroidery designs require bobbinfil in the bobbin. However, there are a few occasions when bobbinfil is not used: for example, freestanding lace is viewed from both sides, so embroidery thread is used instead.

Machine manufacturers make bobbinfil or recommend a specific brand. It is best to stay with the bobbinfil suggested for your machine. Good-quality bobbinfils run smoothly, without any excess lint. If you are tempted by another brand, run it through your fingers and feel the amount of lint that comes off, and whether the thread is fine and smooth. If it is not, the thread will leave an excess of lint in your bobbin area and your embroidery will be more solid.

Although the most widely used colors are black or white, some companies manufacture a limited color selection. If you buy these, check one in your machine to see how well it stitches before buying all the colors.

When winding your bobbin, wind on slow and ensure that the bobbin is evenly wound. Do not top up a bobbin for machine embroidery—the tension from the bobbin must be even. Bobbinfil is not strong enough for construction, so don't forget to change it after embroidery.

SPECIALTY THREADS

Special threads can be used in all or parts of an embroidery design. If they have been used in the digitizing, the design will stipulate the thread. Otherwise, you can substitute normal threads with specialty embroidery threads if you choose, but select them with care.

Multicolored threads

There are two main types of multicolored thread—space dyed and twisted.

Space-dyed threads have been dyed in sections. These can be totally different colors or shades of the same hue. The thread looks lovely on the reel, evenly spaced and very tempting. However, these do not work very well with computerized machine embroidery. They stitch out in clumps of color rather than evenly spaced within the embroidery design. Buyer beware: a practice run is needed first.

With twisted thread, two thinner strands are twisted together to make one. These work very well and are especially good for adding the look of texture and movement to elements within a design. They are also good for designs featuring animal fur and those with a natural theme: for example, a leaf takes on a new dimension when stitched with a twisted thread, since the two twisted colors merge very well and give the leaf added life.

Metallic threads

Less is more when it comes to metallic threads, which are wonderful for adding detail and the final glittering touch to machine embroidery.

Modern metallic threads are usually made up of a fabric core with a metallic wrapping, and are available in many colors, from bright cerise pinks to the traditional shades of silver and gold. Space-dyed metallic threads feature several colors on one reel.

Metallic threads are widely used, but they have their problems and it takes practice to use them. The thread twists as it leaves the spool. When the twists reach the tension disks they cause a blockage, so the thread in front of the twist stretches and shreds or breaks. Some machine manufacturers include nylon nets with their accessories and you can try these to alleviate the twists before they get to the tension disks. Another technique is to put the thread on a thread stand away from the embroidery machine, so that the twist rights itself long before reaching the machine. Reducing the top tension will stop the nylon core from becoming stretched, which results in breakages.

If a digitizer has used metallic thread and it is listed in the color charts you can be confident it will work, since the digitizer will have allowed for the difference between the two types of thread. If you substitute metallic thread for another thread you may have problems because the density of the embroidery design hasn't allowed for it and, as the needle punches the dense stitching, the nylon core breaks, causing shredding.

Slow your machine down to the lowest speed when using any metallic thread. As metallic thread has the nylon inside, it stretches at high speed. Moreover, always change the needle to a metallic needle. Metallics must not be restricted.

Invisible thread

This nylon thread is used in invisible quilting designs. It is a fine filament and is available in clear or light gray. It doesn't show when stitched; instead, the stitches disappear into the fabric, especially on highly patterned fabrics where the quilted effect is more desirable than the stitching itself. It is not very strong and so breaks easily at high speeds, so the machine must be slowed right down.

Shrinking thread

This polyester thread sews like normal thread. The embroidery design is shrunk after stitching and the work shrinks to create texture. A great novelty thread for artistic work.

CUTTING METALLIC THREAD

Do not use your built-in thread cutter with metallic threads, since they will soon blunt it. Use a sharp pair of small scissors instead.

◀ Metallic threads are wonderful when used as accents.

THREAD WEIGHTS

Embroidery thread is available in different thread weights. The higher the number, the thinner the thread. A thread weight 30 is thicker than a thread weight 40. The weights usually used with computerized embroidery are 30, 40, 50, and 60. Most of the embroidery designs you buy will have been digitized using the average 40 weight. If the thread used differs, the embroidery design's documentation will tell you this, either on the paperwork, the booklet, or the color chart. It is advisable to use the thread weight stated, although you don't have to use the specified brand. Digitizers vary in their favorite threads and usually state which thread brands, numbers, or colors they have used. Use your thread spools or your carded thread charts to match the colors.

THREAD STANDS

The thread on a thread stand is passed up through an upright delivery system. The thread feeds evenly off the stand before it is delivered into the threading system on the embroidery machine. Thread stands have a firm base with two or more cone holders. They can either be stand-alone or attached to the back of the embroidery machine. The stand-alone ones can be moved away from the machine when using metallic threads.

THREAD CONES

Some threads are supplied on cones that should be used on a thread stand. Coned threads don't work well on machines that have horizontal spool holders, because sometimes the thread is wound in the opposite direction to suit the machine. The hole up the center of the cone is too big for the spool, resulting in movement, therefore the thread isn't delivered evenly. Upright spool holders on sewing machines are designed for smaller reels, because the spool can revolve easily as you use it. However, 1,100-yard (1,000-m) cones are quite large and heavy. This means that the cone can't rotate easily and thread is pulled tight and stretches as it tries to pull the weight of the cone.

▲ Purchasing large cones of thread makes economic sense but they require a thread stand in order to be delivered evenly.

THREAD CARE

Thread needs to be looked after. Once the plastic wrapper has been removed, it begins to age. The moisture content slowly disappears and the resultant dry and brittle thread will break and shred. Thread fades in sunlight so should be kept out of the light and in dust-free containers. It is a good idea to keep colors rather than brands together in airtight containers. These can be stored away from dust, sunlight, and radiators, and the shades can be seen at a glance.

THREAD COLOR CHARTS

Embroidery designs usually include a thread color chart. If the embroidery design is in a collection on USB memory stick, memory card, CD-ROM, etc., the color charts will be with the design set. If you are printing the chart from a download, first ensure that your printer ink is full. Colors are different from a catalog to a printer. Do not try to follow the chart from a computer screen because it will display differently depending on your computer. Thread numbers are sometimes given with charts.

BOBBINFIL AS BASTING THREAD

Don't throw away bobbinfil thread on a poorly wound bobbin, because bobbinfil is excellent basting thread: it is fine, smooth, and breaks easily.

▶ If you can't find the thread color you want in your preferred brand, consult a thread comparison chart. This will show you the nearest match in other brands.

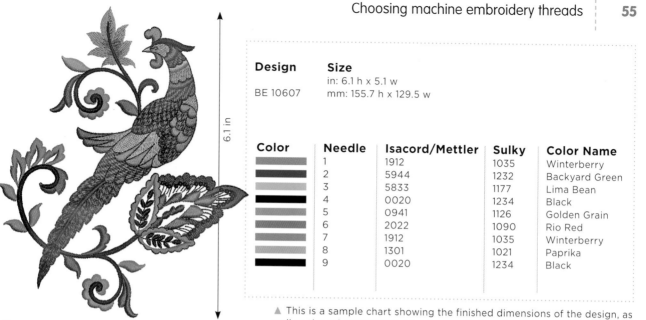

Design	**Size**			
BE 10607	in: 6.1 h x 5.1 w			
	mm: 155.7 h x 129.5 w			

Color	Needle	Isacord/Mettler	Sulky	Color Name
	1	1912	1035	Winterberry
	2	5944	1232	Backyard Green
	3	5833	1177	Lima Bean
	4	0020	1234	Black
	5	0941	1126	Golden Grain
	6	2022	1090	Rio Red
	7	1912	1035	Winterberry
	8	1301	1021	Paprika
	9	0020	1234	Black

6.1 in

5.1 in/ 129.5 mm

▲ This is a sample chart showing the finished dimensions of the design, as well as thread conversions allowing you to buy from your preferred brand.

If you want to switch numbers to a different brand of thread, check the Internet for thread comparison charts, which give alternative numbers to the brand used in the embroidery design.

Thread color charts do not have to be adhered to all the time. If you are sewing a large, intense design it is difficult to make color alterations, so a chart is followed—for example, photo stitch. However, if you are sewing a flower design and don't like the colors in the design, make alterations.

ALTERING THREAD COLORS

Thread colors can be altered on some machines in the editing section. You alter the color on the screen so that you know which color is next. Thread colors can be altered in software and saved before the embroidery design is sent to the machine. Alternatively, line threads up next to your color chart and simply swap one color for another as desired.

NAMED THREAD COLORS

Beware of "named" thread colors on your embroidery machine. Some machines are programmed with a thread collection. Check in your manual to see if you can replace the programmed collection with a different brand. For example, Brother machines are programmed with the Brother thread collections at the factory. The Brother embroidery thread collections have fewer colors than the Madeira range, thus green covers several shades of green in either direction. In some of their machines you have the option of altering the thread selection to Madeira. When you take this option the thread names and numbers will change because there is a wider range of colors for the machine to choose from. Not all machines have all thread companies listed, but in most machines there are at least two or three of the more popular brands.

If in doubt, look at the printed embroidery design rather than the screen on your embroidery machine. Some thread companies name their colors in a completely different way to how your brain perceives the color. "Christmas red" can be any color in the red spectrum depending on who named the thread, and it may not be as you would imagine it!

▼ Thread color charts show the vast number of colors available for that particular brand.

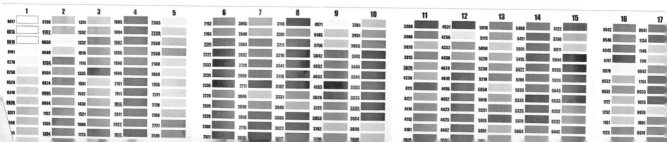

Thread tension

Thread tension has a huge impact on the overall appearance of your machine embroidery. In machine sewing the bobbin and top thread meet in the middle of the stitch, whereas with machine embroidery, the top thread needs to be pulled down to the bottom so that the bobbin thread does not show on the top.

If the tension is incorrect, threads break, stitches loop, and the fabric bunches because the stitches are pulling in too much. Tiny, messy spots of bobbinfil may also show on the top embroidery. Perfect thread tension is when approximately one-third of each underneath stitch is top thread pulled through. Have a look at the bottom of your embroideries and check that the correct amount of top thread is being pulled under.

Most home embroidery machines automatically set the top tension when embroidery mode is selected. There is no need to adjust these settings unless something goes wrong. The inside workings will alter the tension to the optimum setting.

TENSION TROUBLESHOOTING

Before altering tension settings, first consider other factors that may be responsible for poor stitch quality. When stitching is loose on top, try re-threading the machine. When you are changing thread colors often it is easy to thread quickly, and when you do this the slippery embroidery thread isn't pulled into the tension disks correctly. Slowly re-thread, actually feeling for the thread to be pulled into the top tension disks and into the inside hook on the way up. This common mistake is responsible for 80 percent of tension problems.

You could also try altering the thread brand, since not all machines sew with all brands. If the machine doesn't like the thread, the stitch quality and tension will be poor. Is the top thread brittle? Always check the simple things first.

▶ This piece of embroidery demonstrates perfect tension. You can see from the front and reverse of the design that the threads are neither too loose nor too tight.

Next, check the needle. Is the needle in properly? Is it sharp? Is it bent? Sometimes a needle may look fine when actually, it isn't. A substandard needle can affect the overall stitch quality. Change it to a new one and try again.

Check that you have wound the bobbin correctly. A bobbin for machine embroidery must be wound evenly, without any looseness at all. Make sure that the initial bobbin thread is trimmed close to the hole in the top of the bobbin. A loose thread here will set off the bobbin sensors. Check that the bobbin thread is pulled into the bobbin tension correctly. Are you using the correct bobbin case? Some machines require different bobbin cases for bobbinfil and ordinary thread wound on the bobbin. You may have been using a bobbin case for specialty bobbin work and forgotten to change it back.

If all these things have been checked and you still have problems, then it is time to adjust the machine's tension.

CONTINUED TENSION PROBLEMS
If you have too many problems with tension, your machine needs to be checked by a technician. Tension alters slightly after hours and hours of use and can be reset during your machine's annual service.

ADJUSTING TENSION

To alter the top tension, you will need to consult your manual. The tension settings may be on the top of the machine with a dial or they may be inside. On the top, you move the dial up or down; inside the machine, there is a plus or minus tension icon.

Tightening the top thread

There are two problems that indicate that the top thread needs tightening. The most common fault with tension and machine embroidery is the bobbin thread appearing on the top of the work. Little white dots appear, especially with dark-colored thread, and fonts and lettering or satin stitches seem to highlight the problem more than a motif. Another indicator is that the top thread creates loose, loopy stitches.

If your machine's optimum setting is 4, you need to turn the tension dial, or adjust the settings inside, down to 3.9. Then try stitching again. If the problem persists, go down another increment to 3.8. Keep checking between alterations until you achieve correct tension. Your machine has a maximum setting, but tightening the top tension too much will only cause you more problems. The top thread may become too tight and break and the bobbin thread may begin snapping if the pull is too great.

Adjusting bobbin tension

If bringing the top thread down to around 1.0 doesn't remedy the problem, it may be the tension on the bobbin case that has altered. Reset the top tension to optimum and take a look at the bobbin case, bearing in mind that this adjustment is not undertaken lightly. Remove the bobbin case and turn the bobbin screw one degree clockwise—and only one degree. Return to the top tension and begin the whole process again. One, the other, or a combination of the two should work.

Too tight

If too much top thread is showing on the reverse, the top thread keeps breaking, and the bobbin thread snaps, the tension is too tight. The opposite needs to happen. The top tension needs to go up to loosen it, from 4.0 to 4.1, then in small increments until the problem improves.

If making minor alterations doesn't improve the embroidery, have your machine serviced.

▲ The upper tension is too tight here. This means that the bobbinfil is being pulled to the top of the embroidery. There is very little top thread showing on the underneath. In areas around the green leafy stitching, there is none at all.

▲ In this sample, there is hardly any bobbin thread showing on the underneath. There is too much embroidery thread. This means that the lower tension is too tight and is pulling too much top thread down.

▲ Light stitch count embroidery on polyester chiffon, using sticky-backed water-soluble stabilizer.

▲ Polyester crepe stabilized with a polymesh cutaway.

▲ Silk dupion stabilized with a light, woven cutaway.

▲ Upholstery-weight suede stabilized with a light, woven cutaway.

All about fabrics

Choosing fabric to embroider is part of the enjoyment of machine embroidery. It is important to understand the composition and type of weave for your selected fabric before choosing your embroidery design.

When you embroider, you pull the fabric as it stitches. The lighter or looser the weave, the more this happens. Hold a fabric up to the light. If you can't see daylight it is a firm weave. If you can see daylight treat it as a light weave.

You also need to try your best to embroider with the grain or accurately on the bias. If you don't, your embroidery will sit incorrectly.

Consider the weight of your fabric. A lightweight fabric will not hold a heavy, dense design, but a heavyweight fabric will happily hold a light design. Also look for hidden stretch in fabrics. If a fabric has a mix of fibers (for example, wool with 5 percent polyester), it may well stretch. When you hold the weave up to look in the light, it looks firm but isn't. This fabric would need to be treated as a stretch fabric, otherwise it will give and create lumps as it is being embroidered.

The higher the density of your embroidery design, the greater the pull on fabric. As the stitches form, the fabric "pulls in" or shrinks with the stitching. Choosing the correct stabilizer prevents the fabric from pulling in.

AVOID SHRINKAGE
Always prewash launderable fabric before embroidering to allow for shrinkage. Any shrinkage after embroidery will spoil the work. In addition, if you use steam when pressing and there is any shrinkage that hasn't already gone, the steam will do the shrinking and the embroidery will pucker up.

TEST STITCH OUTS
A test stitch out is always a good idea. Record all tests, good and bad, in a notebook. Make a note of stabilizer used, fabric used, stitch count, and any other relevant information. You will be amazed at how quickly your sample book grows and you can use it for reference time and again.

▼ Stretch jersey stabilized with iron-on fusible tearaway and then hooped with polymesh cutaway to support the denser areas of the embroidery.

▼ Medium, woven cutaway was used to support this dense design. A water-soluble film was laid over the embroidery area to prevent the stitches from sinking into the chenille fabric.

▼ Handmade paper laid on top of sticky-backed tearaway, with a light design stitched in cotton thread.

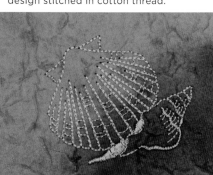

FABRICS, STABILIZERS, AND DESIGN CHOICES

There are far too many fabrics to list them all, but this overview, accompanied by suggested stabilizers and thoughts on appropriate design choices, can be used as a guide. With a very lightweight and light-weave fabric you will need to consider design choice and stabilizer, whereas with firm-weave cotton the stabilizer choice depends on the embroidery design itself.

FABRIC TYPE	CHARACTERISTICS	SUGGESTED STABILIZER(S)	SUGGESTIONS FOR EMBROIDERY DESIGN	NEEDLE SIZE
VERY LIGHTWEIGHT WOVEN: muslin, chiffon, organza, voile	These fabrics are very thin and often slippery. They need to be washable in order to embroider. If both sides of the fabric are on view, use the same color thread in the bobbin as on the top thread. Otherwise, use bobbinfil to keep the design as light in weight as possible.	There are two ways in which to embroider on this fabric. One is to stiffen the fabric, either by "painting" layers of a paste made from **scraps of water-soluble stabilizer** and allowing to dry between layers, or by ironing layers of **spray starch** until the fabric is firm and manageable. Hoop the stiffened fabric with water-soluble fabric, which is washed out after embroidery. The other is to use a **sticky-backed water-soluble stabilizer** to hold the fibers still while embroidering. The embroidery design needs to reflect the weight of the fabric, so have a light stitch count. If the embroidery has too many stitches, the fabric cannot support the stitches after the water-soluble stabilizer has been removed. If you want your light-weave fabric to hang, the stitch count has to be lighter still.	Very light stitch counts • Lace designs • Line designs • Quilting designs without batting • Satin-stitch outline designs • Open stylized designs	Embroidery needle size 70. The needle needs to be small with a sharp point, so that the penetration holes are minimal. If the holes are too big, the light fabric will begin to pull apart around the edges of the embroidery.

LIGHTWEIGHT WOVEN: cotton lawn, cotton batiste, crepe, light silk, silk mixes, rayon, polyester, crinkle cotton, linen, and linen mixes	These fabrics are light and some are loosely woven, but they are able to hold a medium stitch-count embroidery design. Some of these types of fabric can be as difficult to tame as sheers, especially polyester/rayon mixes. Using the method of making very light-weave fabrics stiffer before embroidery always helps (see right).	The sticky surface of **sticky-backed tearaway stabilizer** holds the fibers in both natural and man-made fiber mixes.
		    Sticky-backed water-soluble stabilizer: The sticky surface holds the fibers still while embroidering. The stabilizer is washed out afterward and nothing is left in the fabric.
		    Polymesh cutaway: If the fabric is natural, polymesh will hold the design, support the fabric, and leave little show-through—where the fabric is light so you can see the shadow from the line of the stabilizer around the edges of a design.
		    Iron-on fusible polymesh cutaway: If the fabric has man-made fibers, such as polyester/rayon mix, then use iron-on polymesh.
			Light to medium stitch counts
			• Heirloom designs
			• Lace designs
			• Line designs
			• Cutwork designs
			• Satin-stitch designs
			• Open stylized designs
			• Tone-on-tone single color
				Embroidery needle size 75. These fabrics will pucker and catch if the needle is too large. If the fibers are man-made and the needle is too big, loops appear as the needle tries to embroider. There will be holes around the outer edges of the embroidery, although the fabric doesn't disintegrate as quickly as very light weaves.

FABRIC TYPE	CHARACTERISTICS	SUGGESTED STABILIZER	SUGGESTIONS FOR EMBROIDERY DESIGN	NEEDLE SIZE

MEDIUM-WEIGHT WOVEN: 100 percent cotton, silk dupion, satin-backed crepe, patchwork cotton, cotton mixes	These types of fabric are lovely to embroider on. The embroidery design itself will dictate which stabilizer to use. The fabric holds embroidery very well, and is the ideal choice for beginners to embroidery.	The stabilizer depends on the embroidery design itself. If a quilting design is desired, a **light tearaway** will be sufficient. If an appliqué with satin-stitched edges is the embroidery design selected, a **medium-weight tearaway** needs to be chosen, and so on. If the tearaway breaks down or the fabric puckers, select a **cutaway**.
		   Use the following if your medium-weight fabric has hidden stretch: **Iron-on fusible tearaway, iron-on fusible cutaway, sticky-backed tearaway.**
		   Use the following if your fabric has hidden stretch and you want to embroider a very dense design: **Water-activated sticky-backed tearaway, water-activated sticky-backed cutaway.**
			Light to heavy stitch counts
			• Motif-style designs
			• Heirloom designs
			• Quilting designs
			• Appliqué
			• Fonts and fancy letters
			• Cutwork and cutwork lace
			• Border and frame designs
			• Stylized open designs
			• Denser cartoon characters
			• Fringe designs
				Embroidery needle size 80. Use a medium-sized needle for these fabrics, because the embroidery is likely to stitch on top of stitches, since the designs used can be heavier than those on lighter-weave fabrics.

HEAVYWEIGHT FABRICS: denim, upholstery, cotton twill	These fabrics can take any sort of embroidery design. The fabric itself is densely woven and so can support a high number of stitches.	**Tearaway light, medium, or heavy.** The fabric is strong, so the weight of the stabilizer depends on the embroidery design density. **Cutaway light, medium, or heavy.** If tearaway stabilizer breaks underneath the design, a cutaway should be used instead.	Medium to high stitch counts • Motif-style designs • Appliqué • Photo-stitch designs • Fonts and fancy letters • Cutwork and cutwork lace • Stylized open designs • Denser cartoon characters • Designs with heavier thread • Fringe designs	Embroidery needle size 90. The needle needs to be strong to work through the embroidery design and the fabric. If a size 90 breaks, move to a size 100. If you are stitching an especially heavy, dense design and the needle keeps breaking, try a finer-point size 70. Oddly enough, this works!

FABRIC TYPE	CHARACTERISTICS	SUGGESTED STABILIZER	SUGGESTIONS FOR EMBROIDERY DESIGN	NEEDLE SIZE
STRETCH FABRICS: T-shirt fabric, stretch jersey, elastane	Two-way and four-way stretch fabrics need to be held still before embroidering. The fibers give and stretch unless they are stopped from moving. These fabrics need some thinking about, because the stretch falls into one category and the weight of the stretch fabric falls into others.	Iron-on fusible polymesh cutaway for stretch elastane. It is very light under the elastane. Iron-on fusible tearaway or polymesh cutaway, or any sticky-backed stabilizer, for stretch T-shirt/stretch knit. Use to keep the fibers still. Iron-on fusible tearaway or polymesh cutaway, or any sticky-backed stabilizer, for stretch sweatshirts or stretch denim. Use to keep the fibers still. Any sticky-backed stabilizer for stretch velvet. Use to keep the fibers still and prevent hoop marks. Will need a topping (see Pile Fabrics, below).	Light to medium stitch counts • Motif-style designs • Heirloom designs • Lace designs • Fonts and fancy letters • Satin-stitch designs • Open stylized designs • Tone-on-tone single color	Embroidery needle size 70. If too large a needle is used, holes will appear around the embroidery. If the fibers pull apart too much, try a ballpoint needle size 70.
PILE FABRICS: terry toweling, fleece, corduroy, velvet, faux fur, plush fabric, chenille	These fabrics need special treatment. The stitches fall into the pile, so a special film is used as a topping to stop this from happening (see page 64). A dense embroidery design that covers the surface looks best on deep pile, such as chenille or terry toweling. The pile pokes through the design if it isn't covered properly.	Sticky-backed tearaway for medium to heavy stitch counts. Water-activated sticky-backed tearaway for heavy to dense stitch counts. Water-activated sticky-backed cutaway for very heavy stitch counts.	Medium to heavy stitch count • Motif-style designs • Appliqué • Fonts and fancy letters • Denser cartoon characters • Designs with heavier thread • Fringe designs	Embroidery needle size 80/90. You need to use a larger needle to penetrate the layers of fabric, pile, topping, and stabilizer. Velvet needs a size 70 since, although it is classed as pile, it is a medium-weave fabric.
Leather, vinyl, cardstock, and handmade paper	These require special treatment, and will split if there are too many stitches in a design.	None of these can be hooped with a top hoop. Leather and vinyl end up with hoop markings, while homemade paper and cardstock break and rip. Design choice is limited to low stitch count, so sticky-backed tearaway is sufficient. The leather, vinyl, cardstock, or homemade paper is laid on top. The needle penetrates and leaves a definite hole. If this happens too much, the base falls apart or the leather rips. There is no leeway for wrong choices.	Low stitch counts only • Low-count motif-style designs • Lace designs • Line designs • Stylized open flower designs	Embroidery needle size 70 for leather or vinyl. The needle size is important, because the needle makes a larger hole on these than on ordinary fabric. An old, blunt embroidery needle size 70 for handmade paper and cardstock. Do not use new needles, which will blunt very quickly.

Hooping techniques

How you hoop your fabric depends on your design choice and the types of fabric and stabilizer used. There are two standard ways of hooping, and other techniques lead on from these. All methods described below are used in the Embroidery Designs chapter.

The hoop is the frame that secures the fabric during embroidering. Hoops are not interchangeable between machine brands, so you must use the hoop that was supplied with your embroidery machine.

Machine hoops are made from rigid plastic and are not the same as hand embroidery or free-motion hoops. A machine hoop has a means of attaching it to the machine, and machine brands use different hoop sizes, shapes, and closing mechanisms —such as screws or levers. Familiarize yourself with your machine's hoop embroidery area dimensions, since you need to know these in order to buy embroidery designs.

The fabric and stabilizer combination is held still within the hoop before embroidery can take place. Good, smooth embroidery takes practice to accomplish. However, no matter how well you frame the fabric, there will always be a few natural lumps and bumps. A totally flat piece of embroidery is lifeless, and an impossibility with fabric.

IDEAL HOOPING
Perfectly hooped fabric is smooth; wrinkle free, but not tight in or on the hoop. It should lay flat, without puckers, and with the grain line as straight as possible.

HOOP ON A FIRM SURFACE
Trapping the fabric and stabilizer between the top and bottom hoops must be done on a firm surface.

HOOPING METHOD 1: FABRIC AND STABILIZER BETWEEN THE TOP AND BOTTOM HOOPS

This hooping method traps the fabric and stabilizer between the top and bottom hoops, and is also used for water-soluble stabilizers hooped on their own without fabric.

When hooping in this way, do not hoop too tightly. If you pull the fabric in any way, you distort the grain and embroider on a distorted piece of fabric. In addition, when you pull the fabric tight it stretches. When the fabric is released, it springs back to shape again and the design is misaligned, with puckers around the embroidery as the fabric tries to return to its original state.

If your fabric is too loose, on the other hand, it will slip and the design will not stitch out properly. Moreover, the embroidery foot may catch on it. Keep your fabric smooth and wrinkle free, but not tight.

1 Cut your fabric and stabilizer larger than the hoop. Lay the fabric on the stabilizer. Undo the hoop screws until the top hoop fits into the bottom easily. Lay the fabric under the top hoop. Ensure that the fabric is smooth and wrinkle free.

2 Take the hoop, fabric, and stabilizer and hold in both hands at the sides, either side of the top hoop. Hold onto the top hoop with your forefingers and thumbs, keeping the fabric and stabilizer steady. Do not pull the fabric tightly, but do keep it straight.

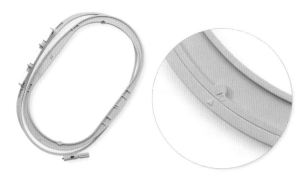

CORRESPONDING MARKERS

Embroidery machine hoops have a top and bottom element, and there is a right way to slot in the top hoop. Check your top and bottom hoops for markings that need to correspond with each other. You then know that the top hoop is the correct way round in the bottom hoop. This is important, because the embroidery area doesn't fall exactly into the center of a hoop. If you insert the top hoop incorrectly the markings on the frame edges, which are used for positioning, aren't where they should be. For many frames, the top hoop easily fits in to the bottom hoop the wrong way round, so this has to be double-checked.

OTHER STABILIZERS HOOPED USING METHOD 1

• Iron-on fusible stabilizers are ironed onto the back of the fabric before hooping. Then follow hooping method 1 to secure the fabric and ironed-on stabilizer between the top and bottom hoops.
• Water-soluble stabilizers can often be hooped on their own without fabrics—for example, when making freestanding lace. Trap the stabilizer between the top and bottom hoops using hooping method 1. When using a fabric water-soluble stabilizer, it is important to use two layers and to hoop the stabilizer straight. For a thick plastic type of stabilizer, hoop one layer between the two hoops.

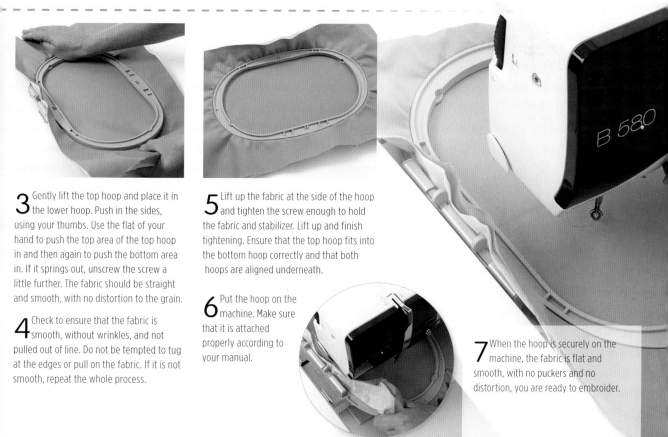

3 Gently lift the top hoop and place it in the lower hoop. Push in the sides, using your thumbs. Use the flat of your hand to push the top area of the top hoop in and then again to push the bottom area in. If it springs out, unscrew the screw a little further. The fabric should be straight and smooth, with no distortion to the grain.

4 Check to ensure that the fabric is smooth, without wrinkles, and not pulled out of line. Do not be tempted to tug at the edges or pull on the fabric. If it is not smooth, repeat the whole process.

5 Lift up the fabric at the side of the hoop and tighten the screw enough to hold the fabric and stabilizer. Lift up and finish tightening. Ensure that the top hoop fits into the bottom hoop correctly and that both hoops are aligned underneath.

6 Put the hoop on the machine. Make sure that it is attached properly according to your manual.

7 When the hoop is securely on the machine, the fabric is flat and smooth, with no puckers and no distortion, you are ready to embroider.

HOOPING METHOD 2: HOOPING WITH STICKY-BACKED STABILIZER

The second method is to hoop a sticky-backed stabilizer on its own between the top and bottom hoops. Fabric is then laid over the exposed sticky surface. The hooping method is not as fiddly as holding the stabilizer and fabric smooth, as in method 1 (see page 62). If you prefer, you can use this way for most of your embroidery. The stabilizer is slightly more expensive than others, but the results are really worth the extra expenditure.

This hooping method is used for difficult-to-hoop pile fabrics (see Hooping Pile Fabrics, below) and difficult-to-hoop areas such as collars and cuffs. The difficult-to-reach section can be positioned on the stabilizer with a template, and embroidered without having to hoop the whole item.

Hooping method 2 is used for perfect positioning (see page 68), because it is easier to be precise with templates when laying fabric over a stabilizer as opposed to trapping it between two hoops.

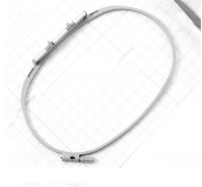

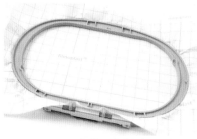

1 This demonstration uses a tearaway sticky-backed stabilizer, which has two layers—a sticky tearaway base and a protective top layer. Cut a piece of sticky-backed stabilizer larger than your bottom hoop. It is a good idea to count the squares so that you know how many to cut next time, which saves wastage. Separate your top and bottom hoops. Undo the bottom screw.

2 Place the stabilizer between the two hoops, with the shiny-coated side facing up. Push the top hoop in and trap the stabilizer between the top and bottom hoops. The top and bottom hoops must be aligned underneath.

3 Tighten the screw and turn the hoop over. Pull the stabilizer taut from the bottom. Make sure it is tight in the hoop. If you tap the stabilizer from the base with your finger, it should sound almost like a drum. It is important that this stabilizer is very tight, otherwise it may slip during embroidery.

HOOPING PILE FABRICS

Pile fabrics, such as toweling, chenille, velvet, fleece, fake fur, and specialty fun fabrics, have a raised surface texture. Trapping a pile fabric between two hoops will leave hoop markings, which are virtually impossible to remove. The light will always catch on the flattened pile, even after washing, and the pile never really recovers from the pressure of the hoops.

With pile fabrics the stitches sink into the pile surface, become embedded, and look unsightly. To counteract this problem, a water-soluble film is added to the top of the pile fabric to prevent the stitches from sinking. The film is left in the embroidery until the first wash when it will disappear completely. The water-soluble film is very thin.

1 Hoop a sticky-backed stabilizer following method 2 (above) and lay the pile fabric over the surface.

2 Cut a piece of water-soluble film stabilizer the same size as the inner hoop area. Lay the water-soluble film over the pile fabric. Pin the film to the fabric on the outside of the embroidery area, around the edges of the inner hoop, to keep it in place.

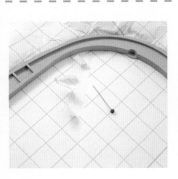

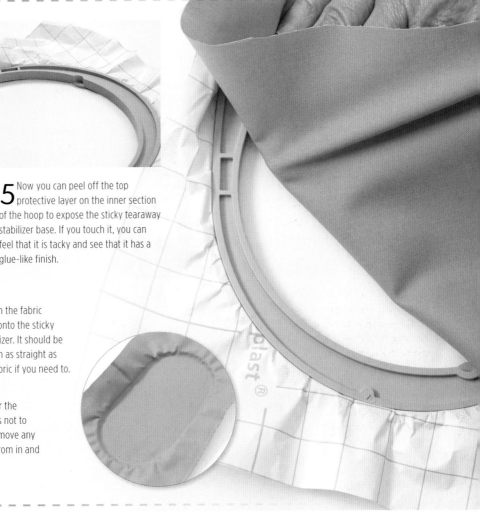

4 Use a pin to score the stabilizer's top protective layer across the hoop. Take care to only score the protective layer, not through to the sticky surface beneath. Insert a fingernail under the top layer where you scored the surface and lift a small part away.

5 Now you can peel off the top protective layer on the inner section of the hoop to expose the sticky tearaway stabilizer base. If you touch it, you can feel that it is tacky and see that it has a glue-like finish.

6 Lay your fabric over the stabilizer. Smooth the fabric without distorting the grain and press it onto the sticky surface. The fabric should adhere to the stabilizer. It should be smooth, wrinkle free, and with the fabric grain as straight as possible. You can lift off and reposition the fabric if you need to.

7 When embroidery is complete, gently tear the embroidery away from the stabilizer so as not to exert pressure on the stitches. Use a pin to remove any excess stabilizer on the reverse of the fabric from in and around the embroidery design.

3 When the embroidery is complete, tear away the water-soluble film from around the design. Wash the fabric to completely remove the film.

OTHER STABILIZERS HOOPED USING METHOD 2

Water-soluble sticky-backed stabilizer is hooped in the same way as tearaway sticky-backed stabilizer, and is used to hold sheer chiffons, voiles, and very light fabrics in place while embroidering. Excess stabilizer needs to be cut away from the embroidery on completion. The remaining stabilizer is washed away after embroidering, thus leaving no trace in a sheer fabric.

HARD-TO-HOOP STRETCH FABRICS

Tearaway sticky-backed stabilizer is ideal for holding the stretch in stretch fabrics still while embroidering, so can be used for babygros, which cannot be hooped.

Positioning embroidery designs

There are lots of ways of placing embroidery designs where you want them on your fabric. Some require expensive accessories and tools. However, the two simple methods outlined below use the plastic template that is usually included in your machine's accessories. If your machine doesn't have one as standard, it is a good idea to purchase one.

PLASTIC TEMPLATES

Plastic templates are thin, transparent pieces of plastic that fit into your hoop. Each hoop has one to fit. They show the embroidery area within the hoop, with marked vertical and horizontal axes, and a center hole for the needle. They have inch or centimeter grid markings to assist with positioning.

These need to be placed the right way up when used for positioning. Double-check that you can read any writing on the template from left to right correctly. When you place your plastic template into your hoop, any grooves at top, bottom, right, and left sides need to fall in line with the raised markings on your hoop.

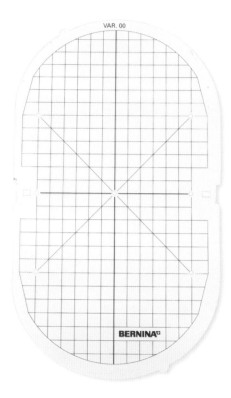

SIMPLE POSITIONING

Simple positioning is the easiest method of placing an embroidery design where you would like it to be, but it isn't as exacting as using a paper template (see overleaf). You will be using the plastic template in conjunction with hooping method 1 (see page 62).

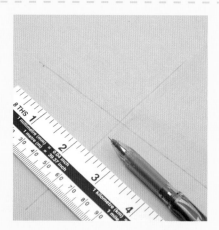

1 Use a ruler and a set square on your fabric to find the center point of where you would like your embroidery design to be placed. Draw two intersecting lines through the center point, using a heat-removable pen or an air- or water-soluble marker.

2 Split the embroidery hoop into top and bottom sections (see page 62). Use masking tape to secure the plastic template inside the top hoop. Pick the top hoop up to check that the plastic template is secured inside the inner rim.

PAPER TEMPLATES

Paper templates are used in conjunction with the plastic machine template for precise positioning. The embroidery design on the template is the exact size that you are going to stitch out. The center markings for the horizontal and vertical axes and the center point are all marked. Embroidery design templates can come from various sources: scanned or photocopied from a larger printed paper template that came with the design set; scanned or photocopied from the design detail book or leaflet that came with a design CD; a

printed-out sheet from an Internet supplier; or printed from software. You do not need to use special paper—normal computer paper is fine.

The paper template is used to position the embroidery design accurately. Some templates also feature color charts, design dimensions, stitch count, and other information.

Remember, if you alter the size of your design, you must also alter your template. It is easy to forget, especially if you print a template and then alter the design size inside the machine later.

ALTERNATIVE TEMPLATES

Clear, printable, plastic sheets can be purchased to assist with templating. These go through the printer and have a sticky backing. They can be used instead of paper and don't need masking tape to hold them down. You can see through the sheet to the markings on the fabric. They can be used several times before you have to discard them.

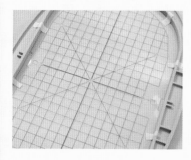

3 Lay out your fabric with your chosen stabilizer underneath. Lay the top hoop with attached plastic template over the two lines on the fabric, matching the horizontal and vertical axes and with the center hole over the point where the two lines cross.

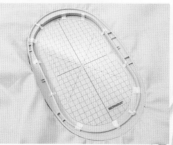

4 Pick up the fabric and top hoop using two hands, one either side, and carefully position it inside the bottom hoop. If it all slips as you press it into the hoop, take it out and start again. Ensure that the top hoop is the correct way up. Without moving the hoop, tighten the screw sufficiently to hold everything in place. Lift up the hoop and fully tighten the screw.

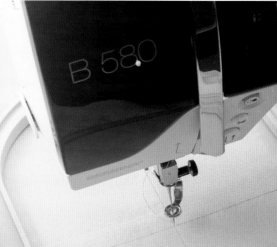

5 Remove the plastic template. Take the hooped fabric to the machine. Load your design and open. Use the positioning facility (jog keys) to line up the center of the crossed lines with the needle and begin sewing.

6 Remove the pen marks using a hair-dryer for heat-removable pen marks or a damp cloth on water-soluble marks.

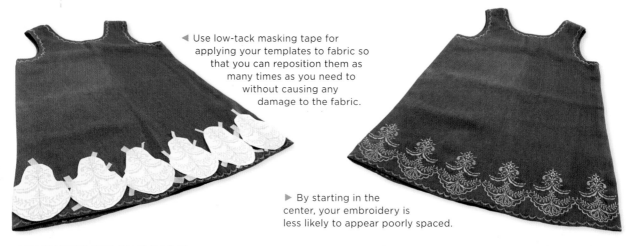

◀ Use low-tack masking tape for applying your templates to fabric so that you can reposition them as many times as you need to without causing any damage to the fabric.

▶ By starting in the center, your embroidery is less likely to appear poorly spaced.

USING TEMPLATES ON CLOTHING

When using templates on garments, make sure you have sufficient templates for your layout and cut them out as close to the printed embroidery design as possible with scissors. Put the cut-out templates on your selected fabric and secure them using masking tape. Place the templates very close to each other, or even overlapping each other if necessary to align the embroideries. When you are embroidering, you will need to fold the adjacent template out of the way carefully. Embroider each design separately, removing each template as you go. It is always best to begin in the center and work toward the edges. The center is the section that draws the eye first and if you go off course as you move further out it doesn't jump out at the viewer quite as quickly.

PERFECT POSITIONING

This method is used with one or several templates for precise positioning. If using several paper templates and the positioned templates on the fabric get in the way of close-proximity embroidery, fold them slightly without moving their position and use more masking tape to secure them out of the embroidery area. You will be using hooping method 2 (see page 64), so need sticky-backed stabilizer.

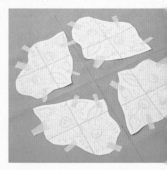

1 Scan, trace, or print your embroidery design template. If you are going to use more than one embroidery in a large layout, make a template for each. Follow the same procedure for every design template in a large layout.

2 Closely cut around the template: don't cut into the design, but do trim closely. If you are templating more than one at a time, it is easier if the excess paper around the template has been cut off. Draw in the axis lines on the paper templates with a pen and ruler to make them darker.

3 Decide where you want your embroidery designs to be. Draw longer horizontal and vertical axes right through the center of the fabric. Pin the templates in your chosen positions, using rulers and set squares and aligning the horizontal and vertical axes on the paper templates with the drawn lines on the fabric. Use small pieces of masking tape to secure the templates.

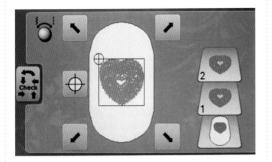

CLOSE WORK

This method will place your embroideries to within a millimeter of where you want them to be. If you are templating embroideries very close together, use the trace function on the machine. If necessary, select the embroidery design and follow through the design using the Needle Step Forward function. This is the same function that is used to reverse when a thread has broken. The only difference is that you are traveling forward not backward. The function can be used before embroidery has begun. Go forward until you reach the point where the embroideries meet.

ROTATING TEMPLATES

You can mirror-image or rotate templates on a printer, scanner, or photocopier. If templating several designs that rotate and mirror-image, don't forget to alter the embroidery position on the embroidery machine screen as well. This is easy to overlook and you end up sewing the design the wrong way round.

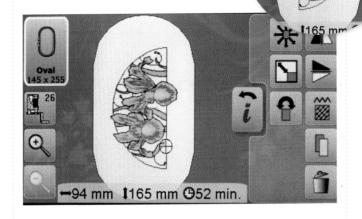

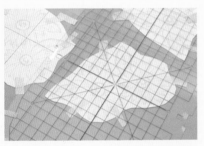

4 Take your plastic template and use more masking tape to secure it over one of the paper templates, matching the horizontal and vertical lines and ensuring that the center point is visible through the central hole. Make sure the plastic template is the right way up.

5 Hoop sticky-backed stabilizer, following hooping method 2 (see page 64). Pick up the fabric and the plastic template without separating the two. Lay the plastic template inside the hoop, matching the cut-out markings with the grooves on the inner hoop. Gently press down on the plastic template and fabric.

6 Remove the plastic template. Take the hooped and paper-templated fabric to the machine and load the design. Use the positioning facility (jog keys) on the machine to line up the needle with the center marking of the paper template. Use the hand wheel to ensure that the needle falls exactly over the marked center point.

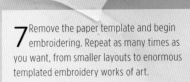

7 Remove the paper template and begin embroidering. Repeat as many times as you want, from smaller layouts to enormous templated embroidery works of art.

CHAPTER 3

Embroidery designs

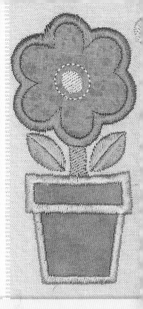

With machine and materials ready to use, it's time to begin embroidering. In the following chapter, we look at an assortment of embroideries, embroidery types, and embroidery techniques, from the easier motif-style designs through to a few of the more adventurous types of design. Taking all the advice given, you should be well equipped to produce stunning embroideries with ease.

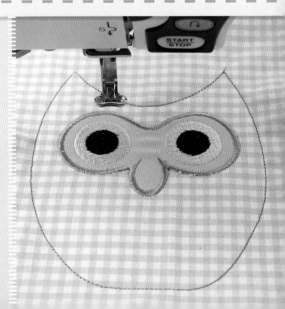

Motif designs

Motif-style embroidery designs are the ones most frequently used with embroidery machines. The subject matter varies according to personal preference and taste. Motif styles are the easiest to master, after taking into consideration stabilizer selection, fabric, and stitch count.

The stitches used are predominantly straight stitches with a minimum of $1/16$ in (2mm) and maximum of $5/16$ in (9mm) stitch length. The stitches travel in different directions—up, down, across—and at different angles to create movement and bring

life to the subject matter. The use of satin stitches in varying widths and lengths also brings texture to the design. Thread colors are used in the way an artist uses paint, to create depth and illusion. The digitizer turns individual artwork into stitches using a software program and his or her own interpretation, thus enabling the home embroiderer to purchase an enormous variety of designs.

BIG AND SMALL

This category includes the larger scenic-style designs with up to 100,000 stitches sewn in the larger hoops, through to the smallest delicate flowers containing around 2,000 stitches. Designs with higher stitch counts per square inch need a good-quality stabilizer, otherwise they will not sit properly, or the stitches will be offline—as with cartoon

EMBROIDERING A MOTIF-STYLE DESIGN

The example is a floral design that incorporates different stitch styles: angled straight-stitch fill for the leaves and satin-stitch fill in different widths for the flowers. The sample shows the way a skilled digitizer can use the same stitches in different lengths and widths for movement and to produce surface texture.

ORDER OF WORK

Color charts often feature the same color several times in one embroidery design. Don't try to jump the colors so that you stitch one particular color all in one go, since some colors will naturally stitch over others during the embroidery process. To try and hurry the embroidery will spoil the design.

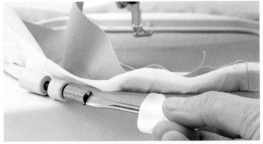

2 Put in a new needle of the correct size for your fabric. Use embroidery thread in the top and bobbinfil in the bottom. Following the onscreen commands, begin sewing your embroidery. Follow the onscreen colors, or a color chart. Stitch the first color.

1 The design example has 20,266 stitches in a $5^3/_4$ x $5^3/_4$-in (140 x 140-mm) hoop space, so a medium-weight cutaway stabilizer is used. Hoop your fabric with the stabilizer. Tighten the screw or hoop closure to hold the fabric and stabilizer in place.

3 Stitch more colors, stopping the machine between each one. The machine will tell you when to alter the color and which color is next. Stop the machine and cut all jump threads as you go. You must stop the machine to use scissors near the frame.

CHARACTERISTICS

- Stitches used at different angles for texture and movement
- Color used for depth and illusion
- Can have a base zigzag understitch to secure the fabric

characters that have a black outline missing the main body. Lower stitch counts per square inch, such as an open, stylized flower, will require a lighter stabilizer, such as tearaway.

These embroidery designs can generally be resized by 20 percent in either direction without loss of quality. When beginning machine embroidery, follow the recommended thread weights until you can see the differences and are better equipped to make changes.

4 After a few colors have been stitched, stop the machine. Take the hoop off the machine, turn your embroidery over, and trim any bobbin threads on the reverse. Put the hoop back on and continue sewing. Note here that areas appear to be unstitched. The gaps will be stitched with a different color later. The machine will tell you when the embroidery is complete and will stop sewing. The last color will show on the screen and the machine will issue a double beep to let you know it has ended.

5 Turn the work over and trim away any loose threads. This is easiest while the embroidery is still in the hoop. Trim away any excess stabilizer with a pair of small, sharp scissors. Be careful not to cut into the fabric. Press on a folded towel, embroidered side facing down.

The term "heirloom sewing" describes a collection of fine hand-sewing and embroidery techniques from the nineteenth and early twentieth centuries. Heirloom machine embroidery designs are beautiful, delicate designs that replicate the original, exquisite hand-sewn embroidery.

Heirloom designs

Epitomized by pale, muted thread colors on white or ecru fine fabrics, and often decorated with French or Swiss lace, heirloom sewing was traditionally used on ladies' clothing and lingerie, outfits for babies and infants, and fine linens, particularly those stitched for hope chests. Modern sewing machines can successfully imitate those intricate hand-sewing skills, using delicate thread colors, exquisite laces, and fine fabrics. The sense of accomplishment and satisfaction to be achieved from heirloom sewing lies in the creation of a beautiful piece, such as a christening gown, that can be handed down through the generations.

Don't resize heirloom embroidery designs beyond 5 percent in either direction, since the fine, dainty stitches used in the digitizing are already at the optimum size, and enlarging or decreasing them will be detrimental to the design.

DISTINGUISHING FEATURES

Heirloom designs for machine embroidery are characterized by dainty flowers, small scrolls and curls, candlewicking stitches, bullion roses, tiny eyelets, and ribbons and bows. Ribbon, netting, or lace are also often incorporated during the embroidery, or added as finishing touches. Other sewing techniques are also classified as heirloom sewing, such as wing-needle sewing, cutwork, candlewicking, and lace shaping.

EMBROIDERING HEIRLOOM DESIGNS

Preparing your fabric and choosing the correct stabilizer and thread is key to perfecting heirloom designs. Keep all the elements as light as possible. Heirloom features in this piece include a pale pink ribbon bow, off-white 100 percent cotton fabric, tiny blue daisies and pink bullion roses, and lighter shades of thread colors: cream, pale lemon, pale blue, pale pink, and muted green.

1 Spray starch the fabric to stabilize the fibers. Use a hot iron and several light layers of starch, taking care not to scorch the fabric.

2 Hoop the fabric with no-show nylon mesh stabilizer underneath. The mesh is a strong cutaway stabilizer, but will not show beneath the fabric. Don't pull the fabric, since this will distort the grain and the fabric will shrink back to its original state when released from the hoop, resulting in puckering.

CHARACTERISTICS

- Delicate areas of stitching
- Lighter shades of thread colors are typically used: cream, pale lemon, pale blue, pale pink, and muted green
- Ribbons, bows, and curly scrolls are prevalent

CHOOSING MATERIALS FOR AUTHENTICITY

Ensure that you use white or pale-colored threads for authenticity. Several shades of the same muted colors are traditionally used—for example, white, off-white, and cream with ecru, or pale blues with greens, lemons, and pinks. While 40-weight thread is normally used, for really light embroidery try a 50 or 60 weight. Use white bobbinfil in the bobbin. If you are altering the thread weight from what has been specified, test-stitch the design first.

Try to use the best-quality cotton, 100 percent cotton batiste, or natural linen. Before embroidering, spray the fabric with several layers of spray starch, ironing between layers and being careful not to scorch the fabric. Use the lightest stabilizer, such as a no-show mesh or a sticky-backed water-soluble stabilizer, for best results.

IDEAS FILE
Graced in petals (1)
This design uses typically pale, muted colors with heart shapes, ribbons, and scrolls with French bullion knots. The narrow satin stitch, triple run stitch, and tiny flowers epitomize the style of fine hand sewing.

Baby vintage design (2)
Introducing slightly stronger shades of color can add a newer, more up-to-date take on the traditional interpretation. By doing this, the delicacy of the stitch remains, but the design has a more contemporary look.

1

2

3 Load the embroidery design into the machine. Stitch the design, using muted colors. Cut all jump threads between colors as you go, otherwise they will become trapped in the stitching. Stop the machine to cut jump threads—never use scissors while the machine is working.

4 Remove the embroidery from the machine, turn over, and trim all bobbin threads while still in the hoop. It is easier to trim the bobbin thread when the stabilizer is still taut.

5 Remove the embroidery from the hoop and trim away the excess stabilizer. Be careful not to cut the fabric. Press on a folded towel, embroidered side facing down.

Free-standing lace

Free-standing or stand-alone lace is one of the most appealing techniques used in machine embroidery. The work produced is reminiscent of that made using nineteenth-century lace-making techniques. Lace can be added to ladies' clothes, home decor, and table linen and heirloom projects. It can be used on its own for doilies, jewelry, and other projects, such as bookmarks.

CHARACTERISTICS
- Light and delicate
- No fabric base
- High stitch counts hold the lace together

Lace embroidery designs are stitched onto water-soluble stabilizer and the work is then washed, leaving light embroidery that replicates the look of lace. The technique is not to be confused with embroidered lace, and the words "free-standing" or "stand-alone" need to be prevalent when purchasing an embroidery design. When free-standing lace is digitized, enough stitches are put into the embroidery design to hold it together without fabric, therefore free-standing lace designs have a much higher stitch count than average designs.

Try not to resize free-standing lace designs, since they are digitized to optimum quality.

CHOOSING MATERIALS
Stitch onto a good-quality water-soluble stabilizer. If using water-soluble fabric, use two layers. If the stabilizer runs into holes, the stitches are misaligned and you finish with parts of the design breaking away. The stitch count is high, so skimping on stabilizer is a false economy.

The intended use will be key to stabilizer selection. If you want soft lace, use a water-soluble fabric. For firmer lace, use a plastic-style Ultra. When you wash the stabilizer away, use lukewarm or cold water and rinse several times. For very soft lace, put into a small washing bag and wash in a washing machine on a cool 30-degree cycle.

EMBROIDERING FREE-STANDING LACE

Lace is very easy to make. Use the same thread in the bobbin if the lace is to be viewed from both sides. Use bobbinfil if not. Bobbinfil produces a softer lace. For a large design, wind several bobbins before you begin. Use a size 75 embroidery needle. Water-soluble fabric has been used in this sequence.

1 Hoop two layers of stabilizer. If your hoop doesn't hold the stabilizer tightly, use 2-in (5-cm) wide pieces of muslin cut the same size as two of the sides of your hoop and hoop with the stabilizer. Keep the fabric even so that the tension of the stabilizer remains consistent. Ensure that your fabric is out of the embroidery area. Follow the onscreen commands to begin stitching.

STIFFENING YOUR DESIGN
For a very firm, stiff finish, after drying use a small amount of fabric stiffener. Make up as directed, paint on with a small paintbrush, remove the excess by blotting with a clean paper towel, and leave to dry.

2 Stop the machine periodically during stitching and remove from the machine. Turn the design over and trim away any loose bobbin threads. Replace the hoop and continue sewing. If bobbin threads get trapped during stitching, it can tighten the lace.

1

2

Lace takes an enormous amount of thread, so ensure you have plenty to hand. Use a 40-weight thread unless otherwise specified. Rayon, polyester, or cotton all work well, with the sheen on the finished lace dependant on your thread choice.

Stitch the finished pieces of lace together with the same thread and a narrow zigzag stitch for trims and edgings. When adding lace to the edges of a project, an edging foot gives a very neat finish.

4 Immerse the lace in lukewarm water in a bowl and swish around to remove the stabilizer. The stabilizer turns into a gluey substance, then dissolves completely. Put into another bowl and rinse again. Do this as many times as required: the more stabilizer that is washed away, the softer the lace.

3 When embroidery is complete, remove the lace from the hoop. Trim as much stabilizer away as possible. Removing the excess stabilizer means that there is less to disperse in the water.

5 Dry naturally, flat on a folded towel. Press with the embroidered side facing down.

Lace motif designs

Fine and delicate lace motifs work especially well on flimsy fabrics, from lightweight cottons through to sheer chiffons, netting, voiles, and organza. These designs are not to be confused with free-standing lace: they contain few stitches and need to be stitched on fabric.

CHARACTERISTICS
• Pretty, light, and lacy
• Few colors in one design
• Work well with pale thread colors
• Raised satin stitches add texture

Lace motif designs work well when there is no stabilizer left in the fabric after stitching. Providing the fabric is washable, sew with a water-soluble stabilizer: all of the stabilizer will be removed and the light stitching in the design will be perfectly displayed. Lace designs stitched in this way on clothes hang well.

Use the same thread in the bobbin as in the top if you are stitching on a sheer where both sides of the design are likely to be viewed—for example, a voile curtain. If not, for a lighter finish, use bobbinfil.

Lace motif designs need a fine needle, size 75, and fine threads. The fabric used is delicate, so the needle penetration holes need to be as small as

possible. Try not to resize designs more than 10 percent, since they often contain satin stitches at optimum length when digitized.

VARIATION WITHOUT STABILIZER
Some lace motif designs are particularly stunning when stitched onto two layers of organza without stabilizer, to produce beautiful sheer lace embroidery. Lace designs with a good satin-stitched edge, such as a circle motif, flower, or butterfly (see Ideas File, right), work very well. These can be cut away from the backing organza after embroidering to create an organza lace motif.

EMBROIDERING LACE MOTIFS

Lace embroidery needs to be light and airy, with a lower stitch count than average embroidery, so that the stitches don't pull or cause flimsy fabrics to hang unevenly or drag.

1 Hoop a piece of sticky-backed water-soluble fabric stabilizer (see page 64). Keep it as tight as possible: the paper topping stops the soluble fabric from stretching. Score the paper topping with a pin. Peel away the paper to reveal the sticky side of the stabilizer.

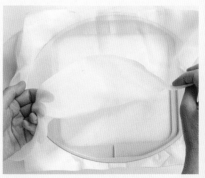

2 Lay a flimsy fabric—here, chiffon—over the exposed sticky surface and smooth out any wrinkles. Try not to distort the fine weave. Press the fabric into place.

EMBELLISH YOUR WORK

Lace designs can look striking when hot-fix crystals or beads have been added as a finishing touch.

CHOOSING A STABILIZER

The most consistent results for embroidering directly onto sheer fabrics are obtained by using a washable sticky-backed stabilizer, so that the fabric doesn't slip in the hoop.

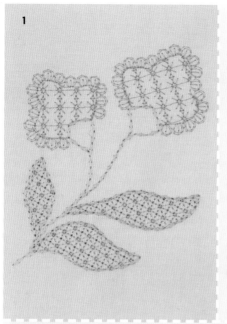

IDEAS FILE

Flower bunch (1) A low stitch count, simple lines of narrow satin stitches, and open lattice lacework make the perfect, quick-to-sew, lace motif design. Fewer stitches prevent filmy fabric from pulling or dragging around the embroidery.

Vintage valentine corner (2) The stylized heart design gains impact from the use of color, delicate design elements, and satin swirls. The design features open spaces, fine fill stitches, and a low stitch count.

3 Embroider out your lace design, taking care to ensure that the chiffon doesn't wrinkle. Trim any jump threads as you embroider so that they don't get trapped in the lacy design.

4 Remove the finished embroidery, turn it over, and trim away any threads from underneath. Gently pull away the excess stabilizer, and cut close to the embroidered design.

5 Soak the embroidered fabric in a bowl of tepid water for at least one hour. Change the water and soak again. Soak a third time to leave the fabric soft and free of stabilizer. Dry the mofit hanging up, so that the embroidery settles into the folds of the fabric.

Cross-stitch embroidery

Cross stitch by machine is fabulous. The look of a hand-stitched canvas can be created in a matter of hours. In cross-stitch designs, the digitizer uses crosses, half crosses, quarter crosses, and backstitch, just as in the hand-stitched versions.

Machine cross stitch looks best when stitched onto the same type of fabric used for hand cross stitch, such as linen, cotton, canvas, or Aida. When stitching onto Aida, make sure you purchase the correctly digitized design with the right amount of crosses per square inch. Machine cross-stitch designs are labeled by count—14, 16, 18, etc.

Don't resize or color sort cross-stitch embroideries. If you want a different size, swap the count. Use average-weight 40 polyester thread. Try cotton thread weight 60 for a hand-sewn look. Use bobbinfil in the bobbin and a size 80/90 embroidery needle.

STABILIZER CHOICE
Cross-stitch designs require strong stabilizing. The last color, the backstitch, will not outline properly if the design is misaligned. Use a sticky-backed stabilizer to hold the fabric or Aida. If the design has a large number of stitches, the addition of fusible polymesh to the back of the Aida helps prevent the fabric from stretching. Baste around the edges, either by machine or by

MACHINE CROSS STITCH ON AIDA

Some design sets come with three Aida counts, so make sure that the Aida and the count on the design match up before you load into your machine. Producing cross-stitch designs on Aida takes a little practice when lining up the needle with the nearest hole to the center. This is necessary in order to keep the crosses aligned with the holes in the Aida. Stitch registration is all important with cross stitch.

1 Hoop some sticky-backed stabilizer (see page 64). Remove the protective surface. Iron fusible polymesh to the back of the Aida. Keeping the Aida straight, stick down, lining up the center row of holes with the markings on the center top and bottom of the hoop. Pin or baste outside of the embroidery area.

2 Open your design. Line up the center tiny hole in the Aida with the needle by using the arrow or jog keys until the alignment is perfect. Double-check by pulling the hand wheel toward you and inserting the needle.

CHARACTERISTICS
- Truly authentic with linen or Aida
- The high number of colors reproduces the look of hand-stitched designs
- Crosses are exactly even

hand, to stop the fabric from slipping. For linen you can use sticky-backed water-soluble stabilizer and wash away afterward for a really soft feel.

JUMP STITCHES
Cross-stitch designs have a huge amount of colors and jump stitches (long lengths of thread left on the surface of the work when the machine "jumps" or moves from one area within the design to another.) Jump stitches need to be trimmed between colors because they are impossible to remove once the embroidery is complete.

IDEA FILE
Bluebird and flower This lovely bluebird is a simple 4 x 4-in (10 x 10-cm) embroidery design that is reminiscent of patterns found on traditional hand cross stitch. The clever use of blue through to gray and white shades on the bird and the dark pink through to light pink shades on the flowers demonstrates how many shades of one color palette are used in cross-stitch embroideries.

PRINTING YOUR CHART
Make sure your printer has sufficient ink before printing color charts for cross stitch.

STAY ORGANIZED
Write the color names—for example, "Light Tan"—on sticky labels and attach these to the top of the relevant thread spools.

3 Stitch the design, following the color chart provided with the design. The list of colors on color charts can be lengthy because several shades of one color are often used. Temporary labels affixed to the threads can make for easier reference.

4 Cut all top jump threads as you stitch. These will spoil your work if they become trapped in the stitches. Remove the hoop from the machine occasionally during stitching, and trim any bobbin thread jump stitches underneath.

5 When you get to the last few colors, sew the backstitches. As with hand cross stitch, the backstitches highlight areas and define elements within the design.

6 Remove the work from the machine, unhoop, and remove excess stabilizer by pulling the tearaway backing and carefully cutting the polymesh. Press on a folded towel, embroidered side facing down. Measure your frame and trim any excess Aida. Frame as desired.

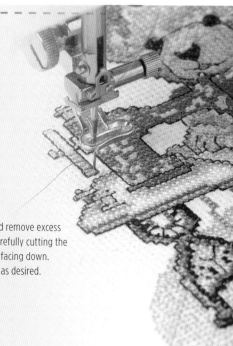

Three-dimensional embroidery

Embroidery designs that produce a three-dimensional effect can take the form of an individual object, or a raised part of a complex embroidery design. The results are absolutely beautiful, and worth the extra effort required.

Three-dimensional embroidery can be very effective. The components can be stitched onto either a base fabric—such as organza—or directly onto a stabilizer, or a stabilizer with fabric, or can be made of free-standing lace (see pages 76–77). The pieces are then put together after the embroidery has been finished.

VARIOUS DESIGNS

The range of three-dimensional designs available to the home embroiderer is rapidly growing, as digitizers experiment with different and new approaches to three-dimensional embroidery. Boxes can be made by embroidering the base, sides, and lid separately, before

hand-stitching them together. Delicate swans, birds, butterflies, flowers, and jewelry pieces are fashioned after the embroidery, and there are even small carriages and strollers available to make as ornaments.

With modular designs, the stabilizing and stitching need to be precise, since the components fit together in a manner similar to models in kit form. Other, less rigid designs, such as the petals for flowers, can be more relaxed in the making. All of the embroidery designs for three-dimensional objects come with very

EMBROIDERING A THREE-DIMENSIONAL FLOWER

This flower sequence illustrates one way to make a three-dimensional design. These designs don't all follow exactly the same procedure, therefore it is essential that you read the instructions accompanying your design selection before you begin work.

1 Hoop a layer of Ultra water-soluble stabilizer with a layer of organza. This stabilizer is thicker than a water-soluble fabric, and some stabilizer will remain in the finished article to help with shaping.

REMOVING STRAY THREADS
If you stitch with rayon thread, you can use a soldering iron to remove stray threads. However, polyester thread will melt.

USING YOUR FINISHED DESIGN
Three-dimensional flowers can look lovely when attached to a hairpiece or corsage.

2 Use the same color thread in the top and the bobbin, because both sides of the flower will be visible. Stitch out one of the three-petal designs and one small flower center design.

CHARACTERISTICS
- Intricate designs
- Made up of several components
- Extra design elements often added afterward
- Can be combinations of free-standing lace, organza lace, or fabric parts

detailed instructions. The time taken to put them together is relative to the detail in the finished project. Some are reasonably simple, others quite complex. Some may need additional parts—for example, ribbons or florists' wire and tape—to finish.

It is not a good idea to resize these designs, because the parts fit exactly as the designer intended. Sometimes, if you resize intricate embroideries, you can alter the shape minutely, and, with three-dimensional designs, the altered sections may not fit.

IDEAS FILE
3-D Marigold (1) This marigold flower is stitched using weave-fill stitches and water-soluble stabilizer. The leaves were included to create a more lifelike flower.

3-D Poppy (2) The components of this flower are weave-fill stitches sewn directly onto water-soluble or polymesh stabilizer and cut out afterward. The effect is much thicker with solid petals and leaves. All solid-motif-style embroideries with a definite edge can be finished in this way to create three-dimensional effects.

1

2

3 Remove from the hoop and trim close to the edges of the embroidered designs, taking away all the excess stabilizer and organza. Trim any threads from the back of the work. Prepare two more sets of petals in the same manner.

4 Put all the sections into a bowl of water and remove a little of the stabilizer, leaving the pieces of the design still tacky. Shape the pieces by lifting the edges of the larger petals and drying with a hair dryer. Leave the small flower center flat.

5 Assemble by pinning the three-petal motifs on top of each other, staggering them so that they don't overlap exactly. Hand stitch using the same color universal thread, because embroidery thread is not strong enough. Glue the center in place with textile glue that clears as it dries. Spray the finished flower with hair spray to help stiffen it.

Crochet cotton lace

It is possible to replicate crochet cotton lace with your embroidery machine. The finished piece looks very similar to a piece of hand-crocheted work using a very small steel crochet hook and thin, thread-weight yarn. Doilies, crochet edging, and even crochet vests are possible.

Crochet cotton lace is stitched onto a water-soluble stabilizer. The best choice is a water-soluble fabric such as Vilene, which washes away easily and leaves no residue. Crochet cotton lace is slightly different to free-standing lace. It is digitized, so the designs have less thread underneath.

Do not resize crochet cotton designs; they are digitized at the optimum size. Use the nearest hoop size to the design size so that there isn't any unused stabilizer to become slack, and only use one design per hooping.

COTTON

One-hundred percent cotton thread gives the best results: cotton doesn't slip and has the required matte finish. Check with the digitizer or company for the recommended cotton thread weight. Readily available cotton thread ranges from 30–70, so it is important to use one suitable for your design. Quilting cotton works well, but you must test-stitch first. Use the same thread in both the bobbin and the top thread. Bobbinfil is not always appropriate because the underneath stitches are not as dense. Cotton thread produces a lot of lint. Be sure to clean the

EMBROIDERING CROCHET COTTON LACE

Crochet cotton holes are very open, so it is important to hoop the stabilizer correctly to prevent misaligned stitches. Use two layers of water-soluble fabric, making sure they are really secure in the hoop. Use a needle suitable for your cotton thread weight, usually a size 90 embroidery needle. For the sample design, the manufacturer recommends cotton weight 30.

1 Stitch the design using the same thread in both the top of the machine and the bobbin. Slow the bobbin winder down so that you don't stretch the cotton. Slow the machine down to its slowest speed.

2 Trim away the excess stabilizer around the design. Trim close to the stitching but not actually touching it. Trim all loose threads.

CHARACTERISTICS

• Stitches look like typical crochet stitches
• Usually stitched with cotton thread
• Lighter and looser than free-standing lace

bobbin area out before starting. If the embroidery is in a large hoop, it may even need cleaning during the process.

TENSION

It is important that the tension is correct and the stitches meet evenly in the middle. If they don't, consult your manual and alter the tension accordingly. Always do a few tests before making a final decision on thread and tension, in order to find the best settings for your machine. If the crochet is too loose, the stitches can fall away or fall into loops.

IDEAS FILE

Rainbow crochet (1) Here, machine-embroidered crochet cotton has replicated the look of hand-crocheted squares. The double crochet stitches and chain stitches plus the use of different color cotton threads looks truly authentic.

Precious crochet (2) This crochet square is made up of chain, single crochet, and double crochet replicated stitches. Squares are easier to stitch together after washing away the stabilizer.

1

2

3 Wash away the stabilizer by soaking in a bowl of lukewarm water. The stabilizer will disintegrate and then totally dissolve quite quickly. Use several changes of fresh water as necessary. When laundering use lukewarm water only, since cotton threads may lose color in the first wash.

4 After washing away the soluble stabilizer, pin into shape on a folded towel and allow to dry naturally. You need to measure the edges of squares or rectangles before pinning and gently pull into shape. Trim away any loose threads when dry.

5 To stitch crochet cotton lace together, or to stitch decorative crochet edgings to linen items, use a narrow zigzag stitch, allowing the needle to swing onto both pieces evenly. Sometimes it is easier to stitch together several pieces before washing out the stabilizer. Alternatively, stitch by hand using the same color construction thread, as embroidery thread isn't strong enough.

Fringe work

Fringe work on embroidery adds texture and surface interest in the form of fringing or looped fringes. Digitizers use the fringe technique to create different effects, such as dress frills and soft-touch animal fur, and as fringed edges and tassels.

Long satin stitches are digitized into the design, and can be several layers thick, depending on the finished requirements. The satin stitches are anchored into the design on one side using a heavy fill pattern, running stitches, or smaller satin stitches. Digitizers can use lots of colors, one on top of the other, for a thicker fringe.

Strong cutaway stabilizer is needed to support the number of stitches in these designs. Use a smaller size 70 embroidery needle for fringing.

This size needle makes smaller holes that will be visible when the fringing is pulled through. A water spray and a gentle rub will remove the perforations and fluff up the stitches, as well as removing any small curls where the threads have been cut and pulled through. Polyester 40-weight thread produces the softest results. Bobbinfil should be used in the bobbin.

Most fringe designs will withstand laundering and wear and tear. However, a little textile glue on the underside will hold the stitches very securely.

CHECK THE UNDERSIDE

For fringing, the bobbin thread is cut on the underside after embroidery is finished, and the thread gently pulled to the top of the embroidery. The underside stitches should be one-third top thread pulled under, one-third bobbinfil, and one-third top thread pulled under. Check the underside: if this is not happening, alter

FRINGED FLOWER

Fringe work takes a lot of thread; make sure enough is on the reel before beginning. The cutting of the bobbin thread underneath requires precision and a steady hand to keep all the thread fringe lengths to the same size. Hoop some strong, medium-weight cutaway stabilizer with fabric. Fringe designs need a good stabilizer and need to be secure in the hoop to stitch out correctly. Load the fringe design into the embroidery machine.

1 Set the machine to its slowest speed. The machine sounds a lot slower than normal, because the satin stitches are longer than average in order to create the fringe.

2 Stitch the whole design out and remove the hoop from the machine. Take out the embroidery and turn it over. Cut close to the white area of the underneath stitches, close to the first one-third of top thread color. Use very sharp scissors.

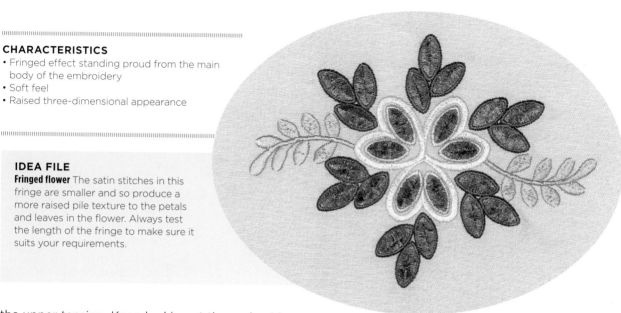

CHARACTERISTICS
- Fringed effect standing proud from the main body of the embroidery
- Soft feel
- Raised three-dimensional appearance

IDEA FILE
Fringed flower The satin stitches in this fringe are smaller and so produce a more raised pile texture to the petals and leaves in the flower. Always test the length of the fringe to make sure it suits your requirements.

the upper tension. Keep looking at the underside until the tension is correct, otherwise your fringe will not be long enough and may pull out.

3 Remove all the white loose bits of bobbinfil, tidy up the underneath, and cut away the excess stabilizer. You will be left with stitches that look loose underneath, but have been secured by other sewing during stitching out. This is where to put the textile glue if needed.

4 Turn the work to the front. Use a blunt tool, such as a pair of tweezers, to ease the cut satin stitches to the front. Do this slowly and gently. Trim any stray ones.

5 Finish by spraying with water to remove any curls or dents in the fringe. Run your fingernail over any small holes left by the needle and fluff up the fringe flowers with tweezers.

Photo stitch

This technique produces a finished piece of embroidery that is similar in appearance to the work of an artist on paper, be it a charcoal drawing in sepia tones or a multicolor design in the Impressionist style. Images are scanned into software that translates the pixels into stitch.

The stitching used in photo stitch is very dense. Layer upon layer of stitches make up the design. The scanned photograph or image turns the pixels into stitches, of which there are thousands. The digitizer then removes any unwanted stitches.

Portraits are superb when stitched with photo stitch, because the detail is incredible. Be warned, however: the first layers of color aren't very pleasing to look at. Be patient and follow right through before passing judgment.

FIRM FABRIC

Use a good, strong fabric with a tight weave. Photo stitch is one of the few techniques that needs two layers of stabilizer to support the stitching. The design sample is of a scene from India and contains 74,000 stitches.

To stabilize the fabric first, use iron-on tearaway backing. This way the fabric can be pulled tight in the hoop without distorting the grain. Then use a polymesh cutaway stabilizer underneath. The stabilizing is strong without being too heavy.

Use new needles every 10,000 stitches. A size 90 is usually appropriate for a firm fabric.

Use the thread weight specified by the design, and bobbinfil in the bobbin.

COLOR CONSIDERATIONS

Neutral colors show the work to its best advantage, and pictures in monochrome or sepia tones are easiest to stitch because they contain only two or three colors. A scene, on the other hand, may include many colors, sometimes the same color

PHOTO STITCH TECHNIQUE

Photo stitch is one of the only areas that requires two layers of stabilizer because the stitching is so dense. The layers of stitch and bobbinfil make the completed embroidery quite thick. Use good-quality, thin stabilizers to reduce bulk in the finished piece.

1 Iron fusible iron-on tearaway stabilizer to the back of your fabric to stabilize the grain. Use polymesh underneath the fabric in the hoop.

2 Line up the colors you will need, making sure that you have enough to finish the embroidery. If you can, print off the color chart that came with the design.

CHARACTERISTICS

- Often used for portraits
- Scenes and pictures similar to Impressionist art
- Dense, heavy stitching
- Incredible detail

stitched several times in different places, so follow a color chart, not your machine's screen. Lay out your colors at the start and ensure that you have a good quantity of each.

STAY SHARP
Change needles often, because the needle tip needs to be perfect to penetrate the dense stitching.

IDENTIFYING JUMP STITCHES
Use a magnifying glass when looking for jump stitches during stitching and in the finished embroidery: jump stitches are easily missed.

IDEA FILE
Green grapes Three shades of creamy yellow and six shades of green were used to create the detail seen here. The design is very dense and so a fusible iron-on tearaway stabilizer was used to hold the fabric fibers still and then a woven, medium-weight cutaway was used in the hoop with the fabric. The basting function was also used to further secure the fabric and stabilizer before stitching.

3 Cut a piece of polymesh and hoop the prepared fabric with the mesh. Pull tightly. The fabric grain won't stretch because the iron-on stabilizer is holding the fibers still. Stitch the first two colors, cutting jump threads between colors. Always stop the machine when cutting threads. The design doesn't look very good at this stage, but don't worry.

4 Continue working through the colors, even though the design doesn't look particularly special. This is how a photo-stitch design looks after the first few colors have been stitched.

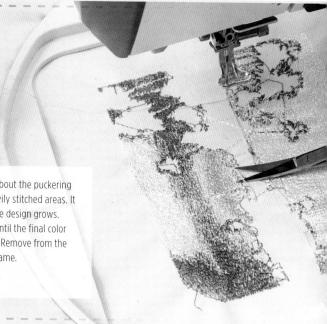

5 Don't worry about the puckering between heavily stitched areas. It will even out as the design grows. Continue sewing until the final color has been stitched. Remove from the hoop. Press and frame.

Line designs

Single-color line designs are the easiest designs to accomplish with machine embroidery. Nevertheless, they are intricate and effective, the details of the drawing being brought to life with the simplicity of the stitches.

Blackwork, redwork, and bluework are examples of line machine embroidery, and have strong historical and cultural influences: blackwork dates back to sixteenth-century Europe, while redwork and then bluework were first stitched in Turkey. Blackwork, despite its name, could be stitched in black, green, blue, or gold.

Line designs use either single or triple line stitch, perhaps with satin-stitch details to raise the design elements or make a part of the design stand out. A sketch or drawing is digitized, and the designs can be traditional or more contemporary in style for the modern machinist.

CHARACTERISTICS
- Simple designs, either traditional or contemporary
- Single-color designs
- Low stitch count, open designs
- Easy to stitch

Blackwork tends to be more geometric, while redwork and bluework are more fluent.

WHAT YOU WILL NEED
Line designs feature low stitch counts, so need little stabilizing. A medium-weight tearaway stabilizer is usually sufficient. If any design stitched runs into thread loops, a cutaway

---

EMBROIDERING LINE DESIGNS

Blackwork, bluework, and redwork are among the easiest of embroidery designs to stitch out. Quick to stitch and effective, with no thread changes, one color remains in the machine throughout. You can sew with any color you please—you don't have to stay within the traditional design criteria.

1 Wind the bobbin with the same color of thread as the top thread. Wind a full bobbin so that you can stitch several designs out without having to wind a new one. The bobbin must be wound properly, since loose embroidery thread wound on the bobbin will slip.

2 Hoop a smooth fabric with a single layer of medium- or heavyweight tearaway stabilizer. Line designs are low in stitch count, but you still need a good stabilizer to support them. Do not pull the fabric: although the designs are light, they will still pucker if the hooping is incorrect.

IDEAS FILE

Butterfly and flowers blackwork (1) This blackwork design has a contemporary look to it and so brings a traditional technique into the 21st century.

Cardinal bluework (2) The simple lines of the bird show how effective one-color line designs can be. Easy and quick to stitch, line designs are very successful in whichever color you choose to sew them in.

1

2

stabilizer will rectify the problem. If you want both sides of the design to be visible, use a water-soluble stabilizer. Loading the bobbin with the same color helps to ensure that the stitches are solid to look at and the embroidery looks good from both sides. Only sew on flat, smooth fabric, because the designs are not heavy enough to stand out against pile fabrics and the stitches will sink. Use the smallest embroidery needle that your fabric will allow, because the holes made by the triple line of satin stitches can spoil the look of a simple design.

3 Thread the machine top and put in your previously wound bobbin. Insert a new needle, because you don't want holes to appear at the ends of your running stitches.

4 Stitch out the line design. The design will stitch quickly. This type of design can also be used for quilting with batting. The batting will give a raised appearance and can look superb on simple quilts.

5 Remove the hoop from the machine, turn the work over, and trim any jump threads. Remove from the hoop and tear away the excess stabilizer. Don't rip it off but tear away gently, so that you don't pull the stitches. Use a pin to lift the stabilizer away in the smaller areas. Press the embroidery.

Embroidered appliqué

Appliqué is a term derived from the French word for "applied." Appliqué, or applied fabric by machine, is wonderful to do. Once you start with appliqué you become quite addicted to the ease of how the appliqué stitches out, and the lovely effects that are produced when combining pretty fabrics with embroidery stitches.

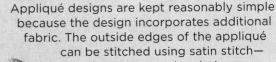

Appliqué designs are kept reasonably simple because the design incorporates additional fabric. The outside edges of the appliqué can be stitched using satin stitch—the most popular choice—or blanket stitch. If you prefer, you can leave the finishing edge off and the design becomes a rough-edge appliqué.

Some embroidery designs will use appliqué in several places, or layer appliqué on top of appliqué.

Appliqué designs should not be resized, because the satin or edging stitches are set at the best width to cover the fabric edges. If you resize the design you make these longer or shorter, so spoiling the finished piece. Use an embroidery needle suitable for your fabric and use

USEFUL TOOL
Long, curved-edge scissors can help with trimming away the edges of the appliqué fabric.

EMBROIDERED APPLIQUÉ

It is advisable to test stitch an appliqué without adding the fabric accents before you embark on a project. The steps for adding the fabric and cutting out the fabric shapes become much clearer with practice. It only takes a matter of minutes if you use just one color of thread for a practice run.

1 Hoop some sticky-backed stabilizer. Remove the top layer and smooth your ironed fabric down. Following the colors from a chart or onscreen, stitch out the first color—in this case, the green leaves. Trim all excess thread as you go, otherwise the loose ends become caught up in the appliqué.

2 Change the thread color accordingly. The next color stitches a running-stitch placement line for your appliqué fabric. You know this by the fact that the machine stops after the row of straight stitches. The example shows the placement line for the flowerpot appliqué. Remove the hoop from your machine.

3 Take a small piece of ironed appliqué fabric and spray a little temporary spray adhesive on the reverse. Do not use too much spray, otherwise you may mark the fabric. Lay the sprayed fabric over the placement line already stitched. Put the hoop back on the machine.

CHARACTERISTICS

- Areas within the design use fabric pieces instead of stitching
- Some designs feature more than one fabric layer
- Will have stitched edgings to the fabric pieces

bobbinfil in the bobbin. Use fabrics for the appliqué that don't fray easily. If there is too much fraying, it is difficult to trim close to the cutting edge neatly. Always use prewashed fabrics, as any shrinkage after embroidery will ruin the project. When the design is complete, use a lint roller to remove stray threads or loose fibers.

ORDER OF WORK

Color charts will feature many more colors than are apparent in the finished design. This is because the digitizer uses color changes to stop the machine for the steps involved. The outline for the appliqué fabric is stitched first, followed by the basting line. After trimming the fabric, the rest of the embroidery, including the appliqué edge stitches, is sewn.

IDEAS FILE

Crazy bird appliqué (1)
The piece uses four different fabrics, all with a small print, and color coordinated. This appliqué sections are sewn first and then the rest of the embroidery is stitched out.

Spring fling border (2)
These lovely appliqué flowers are made up of brightly colored fabrics and clean satin-stitched edges, with fill stitches embroidered on top. The finished effect is fresh, clean, and perfect for spring.

1

2

4 The next color stitches out the basting line to hold the fabric and give a cutting line. This is the cutting line for the appliqué fabric, here stitched in brown so that it is visible for photography.

5 Remove the hoop from the machine and trim the appliqué fabric back to the cutting line, getting as close to it as you can. Curved appliqué scissors help with this. Hold the fabric up and snip slowly to give a neat finish.

6 Put the hoop back on the machine and stitch the next color. This is usually the satin stitch that goes around the appliqué. Some designs stitch a zigzag baste-down stitch on the edges before the satin stitch, some don't.

7 Carry on through the colors. The example has a second appliqué in the design for the flower head. The rest of the colors sew the flower center and the bumblebee. Remove from the hoop and carefully tear off the excess stabilizer.

Quilting designs

Quilting by machine embroidery is extremely quick and easy to achieve. You can use your machine to quilt areas of your project with simple single-stitch outlines or detailed quilting designs, with perfection guaranteed.

CHARACTERISTICS
- Raised areas in the patterns
- Quilting lines are single or triple running stitch
- Can be simple or have added elements for design

Quilting by machine combines layers and embroidery stitches to produce a soft, thick material. The layers are a sandwich made from a backing stabilizer, batting, and a top fabric layer. The top layer can be a plain or patterned fabric, while the weight of batting you use for the middle layer will depend on the amount of loft required. The base layer is usually a tearaway stabilizer, the weight of which is determined by whether the design is of a light stitch count or a heavier, embellished quilting design. You can use bobbinfil in the bobbin or the same thread as for the quilting, and use a size 80/90 embroidery needle.

Always prewash all the fabrics you are using to remove any dressing and allow for shrinkage. The layer sandwich is hooped together and the embroidery design is sewn out.

WAYS OF WORKING
The embroidery design can be as simple or as complex as you wish. Simple quilting designs are outline-only designs, with either a single or a triple run

MACHINE QUILTING

When quilting simple squares, the stabilizer, batting, and top fabric are all hooped together. The method outlined here is the easiest way to make a quilt using quilting designs.

1 Cut out a piece of tearaway stabilizer, a piece of batting, and a piece of top fabric, all larger than your hoop. Try to keep the layers an even size to make it easier to trim later. Layer the base stabilizer, then the batting, then the top fabric to make the quilting sandwich.

2 Open the hoop quite wide. The sandwich will be thicker than normal fabric and stabilizer layers. Hoop the three layers together and tighten the screw.

3 Put the same thread in the bobbin as you are using for the top thread, or use bobbinfil. Sew out the quilting design. If the design is open and uses only single or triple line stitching, it will sew out in a matter of minutes.

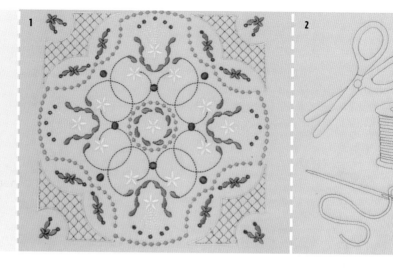

line. They are very effective as either the main quilting design or as a secondary design to others in a project. More complicated quilting designs can use embroidered motifs or appliqué, and can even encompass patchwork in-the-hoop techniques. When it comes to machine embroidery and quilting, there is a vast variety of designs and techniques available.

The quilting can be completed in several ways. The most popular is to make single quilt pieces and sew them together using one of the many quilting methods. Alternatively, you can stitch the quilt together first and embroider the quilted areas on the whole cloth.

BATTING CONSIDERATIONS
Use the batting of your choice, bearing in mind that 100 percent cotton produces less loft than either a polyester or polyester/cotton mix. Always prewash batting.

4 Remove from the hoop and tear off as much as you can of the excess stabilizer. This can be helped by using a metal or wooden skewer to remove the small pieces in the closer parts of the embroidery design. Use a dressmaking pin to get into really tiny areas.

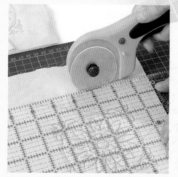

5 Use a rotary cutter with a cutting mat and cutting ruler to trim the quilting square to size. Scissors are not precise enough to trim three layers. Trim the excess threads.

6 Cut away ¼in (6mm) of the batting from behind the fabric to allow for a ¼-in (6-mm) seam in the top fabric.

7 Stitch the squares together with a ¼-in (6-mm) seam. Use a good-quality general-purpose thread. When finished, turn the work over and whipstitch the batting sections together. Now add a quilt backing and stitch in the ditch to hold the layers together. Add a quilt binding to finish.

Trapunto quilting

This type of work is thought to have originated during the thirteenth century in Sicily, and it rapidly became popular across Europe. Trapunto quilting is puffy, decorative motif quilting. Quilting tightly around the motif brings it into relief, and tone on tone was traditionally applied.

DIFFERENT WAYS WITH TRAPUNTO

There are many modern variations of trapunto. Some embroidery designs use areas of tight stitching to create the relief areas. Others use a two-layer technique, where the first embroidery stitching uses one layer of batting, which is trimmed from the back to create puffy areas. Another piece of batting is placed underneath and the embroidery design is completed with closer, tighter quilting stitches. This produces double the loft in the relief areas. Another technique is called shadow trapunto. This method plays with fabric and color. To create the effect, cotton muslin or organza is layered with batting and stabilizer and the raised shadow trapunto motif is stitched. The design is filled with deep-colored thread. A top fabric is then added and the embroidery design is completed by tightly quilting around the raised stitching. The contrast is visible through the top fabric, creating a shadowed appearance. These shadowed areas can either be left as they are or quilted round to bring even more relief to the shadow trapunto. It is best to add a further layer of backing before quilting normally, to secure the layers and finish the work.

SHADOW TRAPUNTO

Trapunto quilting is layered in the same way as normal quilting, but the stabilizer remains in the design, so a fabric stabilizer must be used. In this demonstration of shadow trapunto quilting, the first layer of dense stitches creates the relief.

1 Cut a piece of polymesh, a piece of batting, and a piece of white organza—because white won't fight with any top-fabric color. Layer the stabilizer, then the batting, then the organza to make the quilting sandwich. Hoop the three layers together.

2 Two colors are used in shadow trapunto. The first, sewn onto the organza, is a darker color that will show through the top layer of fabric. These stitches are digitized to create a raised effect. Trim any loose thread because it will show through the top layer.

IDEAS FILE

Dove square (1) The main areas of closely worked, small, decorative quilting stitches surround the dove to bring it into relief.

Trapunto heart (2) This quilt square shows how a simple quilting design can be taken to a new dimension with the raised effect of trapunto quilting.

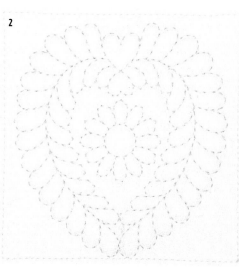

BASE STABILIZER

Polymesh is a good base stabilizer to use in the stabilizer, batting, and fabric sandwich. This is because the stabilizer is so tightly stitched in that it is impossible to remove on finishing. Polymesh doesn't deteriorate over time and becomes a part of the finished quilted piece.

CHARACTERISTICS
- Raised puffy areas in design
- Quilting stitches around raised areas
- Tone on tone is traditional

3 Remove the hoop from the machine. Do not remove the embroidery from the hoop. Spray the design with a light coating of temporary adhesive spray and allow it to go tacky. Lay your top fabric over the design. Pin the fabric at the inside edges of the hoop. This keeps the top layer of fabric stable enough for the quilting around the design.

4 Sew out the rest of the embroidery design using the second color, which should tone with your fabric. The tight quilting stitches around the first color is completed. The relief areas created by the first layer of stitch will play with light as the base color comes through.

5 Remove from the hoop and trim any loose threads from the front and back. Trim the excess stabilizer from the back of the work. Trim the square to shape and cut away $1/4$in (6mm) of the batting from behind the fabric to allow for a $1/4$-in (6-mm) seam in the top fabric. The quilted square is now ready to add to your project. Once the whole quilt has been made, you can stipple quilt between the shadow motifs to give more rise to the design areas.

Fonts and fancy lettering

Personalizing belongings or presents to others with a monogram or fancy lettering makes them really special, and you can use machine embroidery to add decorative letters to lingerie, shirts, or other clothing, or to add a little something to tablecloths, linen, and towels.

CHARACTERISTICS
- Alphabets can be made from popular fonts
- Lettering can be plain or fancy
- Lower- or uppercase letters can be used

All embroidery machines have a small selection of built-in fonts, and you can use these to create monograms of one, two, or three letters signifying a person's initials. Some embroidery machines have frame shapes built in as well, so you have the choice of adding a small frame around your letters.

Machine lettering is surprisingly dense, so always use a good stabilizer: the space between the letters puckers when the stabilizing is poor. A medium tearaway is usually suitable, but for large, thick lettering use a cutaway stabilizer.

When the font stitching is complete, trim the bobbin thread between the letters from the back not the front of the work. The threads ravel if the stitching is trimmed close to the last stitch on a letter. A little Fray Check at the beginning and ends of letters also helps to prevent stitches from coming away.

CHOOSING LETTER STYLES
When embroidering letters try to choose a font that suits your fabric. If, for example, you want to embroider a name onto a towel, you should select a thick, chunky font so that the letters don't disappear into the pile. If you are sewing a delicate heirloom napkin, you can choose one of the more fancy fonts that are available.

EMBROIDERING A MONOGRAM

In this demonstration, a monogram is stitched onto fleece fabric, so the hooping method for pile fabrics is used.

1 Hoop some sticky-backed stabilizer by itself and remove the plastic coating. Lay the fabric to be embroidered over the sticky surface and gently smooth. In this case, fleece is put on the hoop.

2 Go to your machine's editing screen to select an alphabet or lettering. You can add a frame if you wish.

3 Cut a piece of thin, water-soluble film stabilizer and lay it over the top of the fleece so that it traps the pile. Pin the piece of film all the way round, out of the embroidery area and close to the hoop. You cannot use temporary adhesive spray, since it begins to dissolve the water-soluble film.

STABILIZING YOUR LETTERING

Stabilize a large fancy letter with as much thought as a motif design, since the shaping around letters pulls on the fabric.

PLANNING YOUR DESIGN

Test-stitch your lettering before stitching on the item. Depending on the letters you choose, the spacing may look odd or you may not be able to fit your word/name in. If so, try another font.

1

If your machine's built-in fonts are not suitable, search the Internet for others. Check the size of the letters before you buy a set, because shrinking them too much in your machine only makes the stitches tighter and smaller and the underlay thicker.

Fancy lettering is also available as single designs or as design sets. These are letters of the alphabet in upper- or lowercase with extra decoration. They are usually quite large in comparison to fonts, so check the size before buying them.

IDEAS FILE
Floral alphabet (1)
Combining letters with a fancy font from an embroidery design set can make spectacular embroideries.

Victorian monogram (2)
Using a single letter for an initial can personalize a small item such as a handkerchief or hand towel.

2

4 Place the hoop on the machine and stitch out the monogram. The water-soluble film will prevent the stitches from sinking into the pile fabric. Stitches will always sink into pile if a "topping" of film is not used.

5 Remove the finished embroidery from the machine. Cut any jump stitches from the design. Gently tear away the excess water-soluble stabilizer. It will tear easily along the perforations made by the stitches.

6 If you don't want to wash your item straight away, go over the edges and remove any stray pieces of water-soluble film with a cotton swab moistened with water. Rub gently in the smaller areas and the stabilizer will disintegrate.

7 Remove excess stabilizer and thread from the back and press on a folded towel, embroidered side down.

Cutwork embroidery

Cutwork embroidery was traditionally stitched white on white or tone on tone, and used for table linens, cuffs, collars, and frock edges. Today we can replicate cutwork with embroidery machines, and although the technique remains the same, modern cutwork can now include further embellishment.

With cutwork embroidery, a portion of fabric is removed from the design and the cut edges are covered with satin stitches, leaving decorative holes in the fabric. The edges can be left with only the satin-stitched edges, or the satin stitches can cross over each other to form lacy effects within the cut-out space.

Cutwork designs range from small heirloom motifs with dainty holes through to large cutworks with bold statement cut-outs. Some digitizers will finish the edge before the satin

stitching with a zigzag baste-down stitch, while others won't.

PRACTICAL CONSIDERATIONS

Using a water-soluble stabilizer underneath the fabric, which is washed away after the work has been completed, leaves a neater edge to the cutwork than using a tearaway or cutaway stabilizer. The fabric used should be prewashed and shrunk beforehand, otherwise, on washing the stabilizer away, shrinkage may occur.

If both sides of the design are to be seen, use the same color

thread in both the top and the bobbin. If only one side is on view, you can use bobbinfil. Use very sharp, curved-blade scissors to cut the portion of fabric away, so that you have a neat edge for the satin stitches to cover. Use an embroidery needle suitable for the fabric you are using.

EMBROIDERING CUTWORK

Cutwork embroidery designs stitch the part of the design that needs to be cut out first. The fabric is then removed from the inside of the running-stitch shape.

1 Prewash and shrink your fabric. Hoop with a layer of water-soluble stabilizer—fabric or plastic—underneath the fabric. Ensure that both layers are smooth in the hoop. Thread the machine as required.

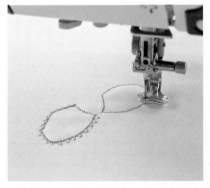

2 Sew out the first color. This will be the cutting line for your cutwork area and is shown on the screen in a different color to the main embroidery color. Digitizers use changes of color to tell the machine to stop. Use the main color for the embroidered cutting line.

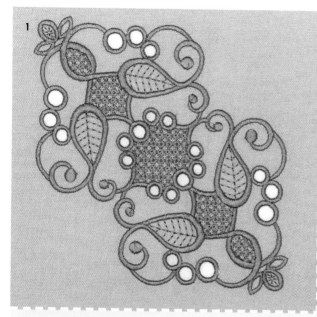

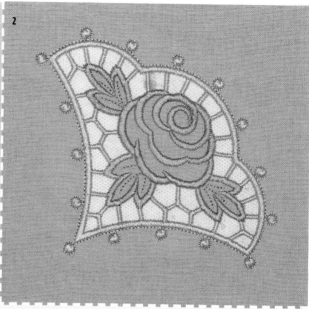

IDEAS FILE

Decorative leaf cutwork (1) The embroidery itself takes center stage in this design; the holes are kept small and neat as added design details.

Rose cutwork (2) The amount of cutwork in this embroidery is significant in comparison to the design size. The cutwork completely surrounds the central rose motif and is joined with interconnecting rows of satin stitch.

3 Remove the hoop from the machine. Take a tiny snip into the area to be trimmed. Holding curved-blade scissors at an angle, "lift" the scissor points and trim away the fabric, as close to the running stitches as possible, being careful not to cut into the stabilizer underneath.

4 Replace the hoop on the machine and follow the embroidery design. If the embroidery design is large, you may come across more areas to be cut, in which case the machine will stop automatically, leaving a new running-stitch shape.

5 Remove the finished embroidery from the hoop and trim any excess threads. Trim as much of the stabilizer away as possible, since it is easier to wash if the excess stabilizer has been removed prior to soaking.

6 Wash the fabric several times in a bowl of lukewarm water to remove the stabilizer. Once the stabilizer has been washed away, neat cutaway areas will appear. Dry the fabric and press the embroidery on a folded towel, embroidered side down.

Border and frame designs

Borders and frames often enhance a piece of embroidery. A border around the edges of a tablecloth, for example, framing centrally embroidered motifs, can be a stunning addition and worth the extra effort.

Many embroidery collections include border or frame designs to use in conjunction with the other designs in the set. Other collections solely feature borders or frames to use on their own or with other embroideries. Design styles featured in this section of the book can form the basis of border designs, such as appliqué, cutwork, fill or line

designs, and borders for quilting or heirloom projects. You can find a border or frame to suit almost any purpose or technique you require.

Use an embroidery needle of a size suitable for the fabric and design selected. The thread will depend on the design. Until you become used to the method, it is a good idea to use a sticky-

backed stabilizer, whether water-soluble or tearaway.

LINING UP

It is of paramount importance that borders and frames line up with the motifs they frame or border, whether that be in a straight row or surrounding a centrally placed motif. This process is not as daunting as it

CHARACTERISTICS
- Borders are long, thin designs
- Frames tend to be symmetrical
- Corner designs are specifically left or right and can be flipped, rotated, and turned for the other corners

EMBROIDERING BORDERS

Borders and frames need to be correctly positioned on the fabric so that they line up or frame a design perfectly centrally. Use the templating method detailed on page 68 to line up two border designs.

1 To stitch a border design, you need a straight piece of fabric. Decide how far in from the edge you would like your border to be. Print templates of your border design onto paper. Cut around the templates, close to the printed stitches. Cut the ends of the templates straight.

2 Place the templates on the fabric, ensuring that the lines on the template are parallel to the fabric edges by measuring from the cut edge to the center line of the template. Fix the templates to the fabric using small pieces of 1/4in (6mm) quilter's marking tape or low-tack masking tape.

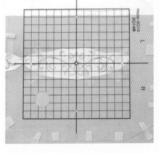

3 Lay the plastic template that comes with your hoop over the templates, aligning the top and bottom marks on the plastic template with the top and bottom of the border design. Use quilter's tape to hold the plastic template in place on the fabric. If you are working close to the edge of your fabric, the plastic template may overhang the fabric edges.

PLANNING YOUR BORDER

If measuring a border on a tablecloth or long edge, decide how many repeats you will need and reduce or increase the size of the design accordingly, to ensure the border fits the required space. Measure the total length. Allow $\frac{1}{32}-\frac{1}{16}$in (1–2mm) between designs and divide the total length by design length plus allowances.

IDEAS FILE
Victorian frame (1)
Stitching a complete frame will enhance simple embroidery.

Canterbury corner (2)
Corner designs can be combined with borders or left on their own.

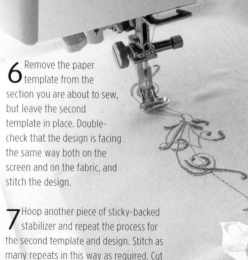

sounds if you follow the templating method described on page 68. There are various implements on the market to assist with templating techniques, but this basic method works every time if followed carefully and precisely.

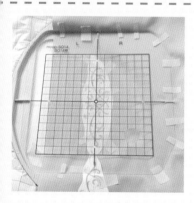

4 Hoop some sticky-backed stabilizer and peel off the protective layer. Lay the templated fabric over the stabilizer and fit into the hoop markings top and bottom. The fabric may not cover the whole piece of stabilizer if you are working on the edge of the fabric.

5 Remove the top plastic template, leaving the paper templates in place. Take the hoop to the machine and load your design. Using your jog keys, line the center point of the first template up with the needle point. Make sure the needle is directly over the center of the template.

6 Remove the paper template from the section you are about to sew, but leave the second template in place. Double-check that the design is facing the same way both on the screen and on the fabric, and stitch the design.

7 Hoop another piece of sticky-backed stabilizer and repeat the process for the second template and design. Stitch as many repeats in this way as required. Cut all jump threads, remove the excess stabilizer, and press.

In-the-hoop project

In-the-hoop designs are simple, complete projects made in the hoop. They can range from small purses and hanging sachets to the more complicated boxes and fabric bowls. Fun to create, in-the-hoop designs give instant satisfaction to creative sewers.

A digitized in-the-hoop design will include lines of stitching that you would otherwise do on a standard sewing machine. Embellishment is usually added to the project using embroidery during the process, whether it be a small flower on a purse, initials on a wallet, or cross stitch on an eyeglass case. The project is then finished. Occasionally a small amount of hand-sewing afterward is required, such as closing the gap and sewing on the feet of the owl in the demonstration below. Other in-the-hoop projects, such as door hangers, tablemats, and baby bibs, don't require extra stitching on finishing.

IN-THE-HOOP PARTICULARS

All in-the-hoop projects come with a full set of instructions. These need to be read before you embark on the project to familiarize yourself with the work in progress. Some use tearaway stabilizer, others fusible, others cutaway. If the stabilizer is to be left inside the project, cutaway is the best option.

Always use good-quality thread and fabric, since the project usually needs to be strong. If the lines of stitching seem weak, use general-purpose thread for the stitching lines both in the top and the bobbin, since this is stronger than embroidery thread and bobbinfil.

IN-THE-HOOP TOY

The instructions for your particular project may be different from those demonstrated in this small, stuffed-owl toy, but the principle is the same. Always read your instructions through first. If your project does not specify a type of stabilizer, use a cutaway one, which will remain intact in the project, whereas other stabilizers will deteriorate over time.

1 Hoop some cutaway stabilizer by itself. The first stitches of in-the-hoop designs set the placement within the hoop. Stitch out the first color directly onto the stabilizer. The instructions for this project state that the placement line is for the base fabric.

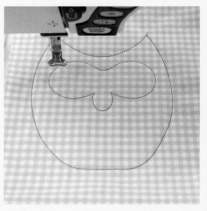

2 Lay the base fabric—for the body of the owl—over the placement line. Stitch the next color—in this case, the outline of the owl edges. Stitch all the lines for this fabric, which in this case also include the placement line for appliqué eyes.

CHARACTERISTICS
- Small finished project
- Motif embroideries can embellish the finished project
- Wide variety of projects available
- Made up of components stitched in the hoop

HOOP SIZES
When buying in-the-hoop designs, double-check your hoop sizes before purchasing. They all specify a minimum hoop size.

PRACTICE MAKES PERFECT
Practice makes in-the-hoop projects easier. As you complete them, the process involved becomes more logical and you can then add or subtract elements as you please.

IDEAS FILE
Gift card holder (1): This pretty little purse is made completely in the hoop. The appliqué is completed before the purse is made up and the ribbon is added afterward.

Cupcake wrapper (2): This is a great in-the-hoop project. Once cut out and trimmed, it is then assembled around a cupcake by means of the little tag slotting into the buttonhole.

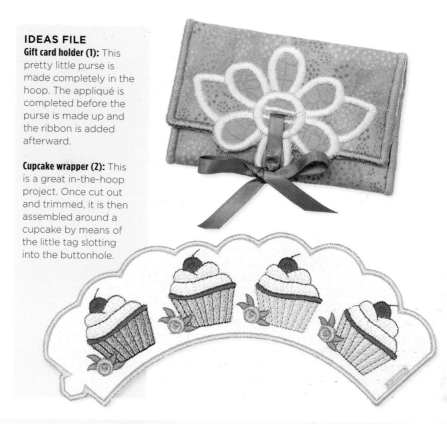

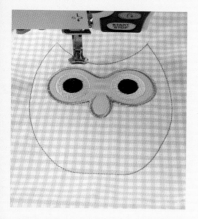

3 Follow the appliqué process to place the fabric for the owl's eyes. Follow through the next colors according to your machine and your project's instructions. The next colors in the sample will be the satin stitches around the eye fabric and the owl eye centers.

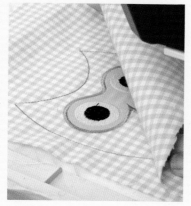

4 Once the eyes are complete, appliqué wings are added. The next step is to lay the final piece of fabric, right side down, over the stitched owl. The last color will stitch this fabric to the base fabric, leaving a gap for stuffing.

5 Remove the work from the hoop and trim around the owl's outer edges. Trim close to the stitching. Clip into all the curves and trim across the eyes. Turn through. Stuff with toy stuffing and close the gap by hand sewing.

6 Make the feet by the same method, using appliqué fabric directly onto the stabilizer. Trim around the feet. If there are any white pieces of stabilizer showing, color them with a fabric pen. Stitch the feet onto your owl.

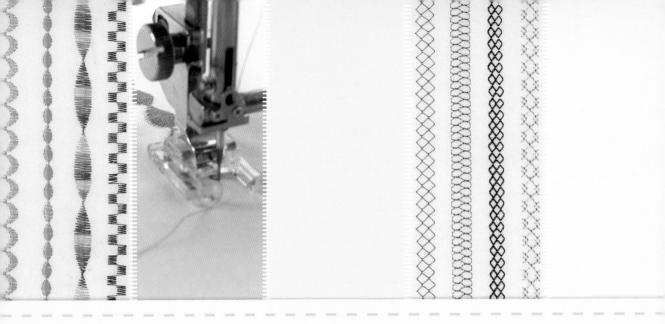

CHAPTER 4

Decorative stitches

All sewing machines feature stitches that can be classed as decorative. A starter machine will have a straight stitch and zigzag stitch, while a top-of-the-range sewing or embroidery machine will have lots more to choose from. Although these stitches are often pushed aside in favor of other techniques, learning how to make the most of them will open up new realms of possibility for the earnest stitcher.

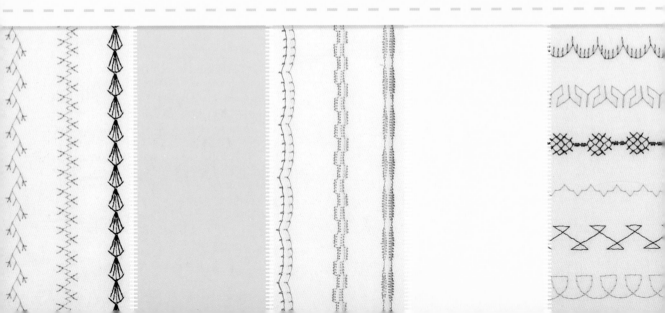

Decorative stitching preparation: 10 steps

Sewing with decorative stitches is often referred to as machine embroidery, because most of the time the stitches use machine embroidery threads. When sewing decorative stitches, there are a few guidelines to be followed to produce the best results. Over and above the few rules of thumb, experiment with your stitches and have fun.

Stitches are stored in the embroidery machine in categories such as utility, which includes straight stitch and zigzag; heirloom; quilting; satin stitch; decorative; and, in more advanced machines, pictograph and other larger picture-style stitches. If your machine includes these picture-style stitches, it may also have a special foot to accommodate them. Some computerized machines will also have fonts built in to this section.

Decorative stitches are very useful for adding finishing touches or borders, and can be used in samplers or instead of a traditional topstitch. They are used extensively in heirloom sewing, especially with twin needles and wing needles. Quilting-style decorative stitches are used to stitch quilts together and are marvelous for crazy patchwork and crazy quilting, and as decorative seam lines.

1

THE NEEDLE PLATE
This is the metal plate that covers the bobbin area. The zigzag needle plate must be in position for decorative stitching, not the single needle plate with a single hole for straight stitching: you will break your needles if you forget to switch plates. Newer machines are fitted with the zigzag needle plate when shipped.

2

DECORATIVE STITCH SIZE
The greatest width of decorative stitching is determined by the width of the hole in the needle plate and the machine itself, usually between 1/4in (6mm) and 3/8in (9mm). When a stitch is selected and sewn, the needle will swing automatically from one side to the other. With some decorative stitches the fabric will want to move backward to form part of the stitch, and this should be allowed to happen naturally. Always allow the fabric to feed through as it wants to.

The width of each stitch is set at a default, which can be adjusted using a dial or onscreen. The width will go as far up as your machine will allow and down to the smallest width that the chosen stitch will stitch out at.

The stitch length can be adjusted to be longer or shorter, and the density of the stitch will alter at the same time. If the stitch is to be made shorter, the number of stitches per millimeter will increase. Conversely, if the stitch is made longer, the number of stitches per millimeter will decrease. For example, a zigzag stitch will become a dense satin stitch if the length is decreased, because the stitches will sew closer together.

3

WHICH FOOT?
The foot you use is important. All machines have a zigzag foot that allows the needle to swing from one side of the hole in the needle plate to the other. Use this foot to begin with.

Open toe foot
If you find that you use decorative stitches a lot, invest in an open toe foot. This is similar to a zigzag foot but is open at the front to allow for more visibility, so you can see the stitch forming and where you are going. The foot has two long toes on each side to hold the fabric. It has an open groove or channel on the base to allow the foot to glide easily over the decorative stitches as they are sewn.

▶ Open toe foot

Clear open toe foot
This clear foot allows you to see everything, without obstructions.

◀ Clear open toe foot

Appliqué foot
This foot is similar to the open toe foot and can be used for decorative sewing. However, the end isn't always open and the foot is often shorter, so an appliqué foot doesn't allow the same visibility as an open toe foot.

WHICH STABILIZER?

Use a stabilizer when sewing decoratively, even with a straight stitch, since the stabilizer prevents the fabric from becoming scrunched up and trapped in the feed dogs. A lightweight, tearaway stabilizer is usually chosen, with the fabric laid on top. Using temporary adhesive spray to hold the stabilizer and fabric together means that you don't need to hold the two layers by hand, and can watch the stitching without being distracted. If you are decorative stitching on light fabric, sheers, or fine heirloom sewing, use a water-soluble stabilizer instead. Tear or remove excess stabilizer between rows as you go. This stops too much stabilizer becoming trapped in the work, which is time-consuming to remove with a pin afterward.

WHICH THREAD?

Any thread can be used for decorative sewing, from all-purpose sewing thread, embroidery threads—including variegated and space-dyed threads—through to specialty topstitching threads. Experiment and keep a book of samples to refer back to at a later date.

Bobbinfil

Bobbinfil is used for as many decorative stitches as possible, the only exception being on a project where both sides of the stitches will be on view. Not only is bobbinfil cost effective, but the finished stitch is also light on the fabric.

STITCH BALANCE

Always practice a decorative stitch before using it on a project, making sure that the stitch is even. On newer machines this is automatic; on older or smaller machines, however, there may be a dial to turn to alter the balance. Turn this dial up or down to adjust the stitch until you are pleased with how it looks.

WHICH NEEDLE?

As with all machine embroidery, for decorative stitching the fabric determines the size of the needle. This, in turn, guides your choice of thread (see pages 52–55).

Embroidery needle

The majority of decorative stitching is sewn using an embroidery needle. An embroidery needle is manufactured to ensure the smooth running of embroidery thread (see page 50).

Metallic needle

If you are sewing using metallic thread, all of the same guidelines for embroidery needles apply to metallic needles (see page 51).

Twin needle

The twin needle produces two lines of identical stitches, and the width of each of the identical rows is determined by the width of the hole in the needle plate. If you use a straight stitch, you can use a wider twin needle. If you choose a zigzag or decorative stitch, you need to choose a narrower gap between the two eyes so that your twin needle has room to swing. Your decorative stitch also has to be decreased in width to allow for this.

Practice first. Insert the needle and thread for twin-needle sewing. Select a stitch and take it down to its narrowest point. Turn the hand wheel toward you to see how the needles swing in the needle plate. If they catch on the plate, the decorative stitch is too wide to use with that size of needle, so change the needle size and try again. If it still hits the needle plate, then use another decorative stitch.

If the twin needle doesn't hit the plate, you can continue widening the stitch in small increments until it is as wide as the twin needle will allow. Remember that twin needles are bought in different widths, so a stitch width that suits a 2.0mm twin needle won't necessarily suit a 3.0mm twin needle. Practice the stitch until you are happy with it, and when you are, stitch a sample and make notes on the stitch width and width of the twin needle used.

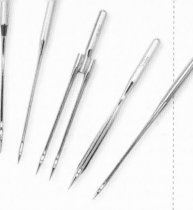

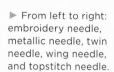

▶ From left to right: embroidery needle, metallic needle, twin needle, wing needle, and topstitch needle.

Some machines will not allow you to select a stitch that is not suitable for twin-needle sewing. If your machine doesn't tell you, use the hand wheel to check. Twin needles are expensive things to keep breaking because you forgot to check.

Wing needle

Using a wing needle with decorative stitches is rewarding. The tiny holes add to the decoration. Make sure that you practice your stitches first. Choose stitches that are not satin stitches, since these will produce far too many holes. Ideally, you should choose a stitch with steady swing and not too many needle penetrations in the fabric. The heirloom, quilting, and simple decorative stitches produce the best results.

Topstitch needle

Use a topstitch needle where the thread is too thick for an embroidery needle. This would apply, for example, to edging a cuff with a decorative stitch using topstitch thread. Topstitch thread is thick, usually size 30, so the stitch is more prominent.

8 TENSION SETTINGS

Decorative stitches sometimes produce crossed threads underneath where the needle swings from one part of the stitch to another. If the lower tension is too tight, the crossed threads pull and the stitch doesn't sit flat and smooth.

If the tension is too loose, the top threads are loose and the threads lift away from the fabric. If either happens, adjust the tension up or down accordingly.

9 PRESSURE SETTINGS

Pressure refers to the amount of force that the machine puts on the presser foot to hold the fabric during sewing. Too much pressure and the fabric doesn't feed at all; too little and it slips around under the foot.

Begin with the correct pressure setting for normal embroidery sewing, referring to the manual to ascertain the right setting and how to alter it if necessary. The pressure is set at default in ordinary sewing machines and automatically/manually adjusts in embroidery machines, depending on stitch selection and fabric choice. The pressure only needs to be looked at when stitching very thin or very thick, upholstery-weight, fabric.

If your fabric isn't feeding as smoothly as you want, alter the top pressure on the machine. Don't forget to switch the pressure back to default or normal sewing after the decorative stitch has been sewn. Newer sewing machines have automatic fabric sensor systems, which automatically set themselves or recommend a setting based on fabric choice.

10 STITCH COMBINATIONS

Computerized machines will allow you to make new stitch combinations, by programming a row of stitches using different decorative stitches. An example would be a child's name with three hearts. Program three hearts, then each letter of the name, leaving the appropriate spaces with the space key. The combination will be stitched as hearts, name, hearts, name, and so on. You can save stitch combinations into the memory of a computerized sewing machine for use another time.

Using decorative embroidery stitches

When making up a project, put the decorative stitches on before the finishing seams. This makes them easier to stitch. If you are decorating a project after making up—for example, around the finished hem of a dress—begin and finish on a seamline. When using decorative stitches and a circular attachment, gently guide the feed to make sure the last stitch fits in.

STITCHING IN A LINE

Decorative stitches sew in a straight line downward, even if you intend to turn the finished piece 90 degrees so that the stitches are going across.

Draw a line or lines on your fabric. Attach the stabilizer to the fabric and begin sewing. As you sew, try to watch the drawn line and center foot marking rather than the needle or fabric movement. With some stitches the fabric is fed backward, forward, and to both sides and back again while the stitch is forming. If you learn to watch the drawn line rather than this movement and keep the end of the stitch consistent with the drawn line and center foot markings, your decorative stitches will be straight.

STITCHING ROWS

When sewing parallel or mirror-imaged rows, stop every so often and check that the stitches are still forming opposite or next to each other. If not, gently pull or stop the fabric feed until the stitches are back in line. One or two stitches that are out of line won't show, but a whole row will.

STITCHING FIXED LENGTHS

In some machines you can set the length of the row in millimeters, choose your stitch, and the machine will calculate and sew the specified stitch distance perfectly. However, most people will need to do some simple mathematical working out.

1 Test stitch on a scrap of fabric and watch where the stitch begins and ends.

2 Measure the length of one complete stitch. If the stitch is too short, sew two and call it one. For example, two stitches combined measure 1in (25mm).

USING A CIRCULAR ATTACHMENT

To sew perfect circles you need to use an accessory called a circular attachment, which fits onto the needle plate. These attachments are not interchangeable between brands because the distance between the needle plate holes or fixings varies between machines.

Always use a stabilizer, otherwise your fabric will bunch up. Using an iron-on stabilizer such as fusible tearaway or fusible polymesh cutaway means that you don't need to worry about the stabilizer moving, so you can watch the stitching.

Use forward-motion decorative stitches only. Stitches that go backward at any point cannot be used.

1 Take one piece of fabric and stabilize it on the reverse.

2 Fit the circular attachment to the machine. The marker slides up and down to the required diameter for your circle.

3 With the attachment is a small pin, and a place on the marker where the pin fits. With the fabric right side facing, position the pin in the center of the circle, then push it through the fabric and into the pinhole on the attachment. Set the marker to the required distance from the center point. Set the machine to the chosen decorative stitch, with thread in the top and bobbinfil in the bottom. Use a foot suitable for decorative stitches.

4 The fabric moves in a circle. Sew the circle, supporting the fabric with your hand and working slowly. When finished, stop the machine and cut long threads—these can be pulled to the back later. If you prefer, you can put the fabric and stabilizer into a hoop to hold it taut. You may have to remove the foot to slide the hoop under if your machine doesn't have a double-lift presser foot.

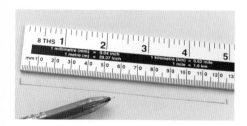

3 Measure your line and ensure it is a multiple of the stitch length established in step 2. If you are only $1/32$–$1/16$in (1–2mm) out, you can stretch the last stitch by gently pulling on the fabric. If it doesn't fit by more than $1/32$–$1/16$in (1–2mm), either lengthen or shorten the line or adjust the stitch length to make the multiples fit.

4 When sewing multiple rows, make sure you begin at the start of a stitch, otherwise parallel rows won't be even. Some machines have a reinforce at the beginning to stop the thread from raveling and a finish button so that your stitch finishes exactly at the end. Press these when you are on your first and last stitch. Match the beginning of the line with the center marking of the open toe foot.

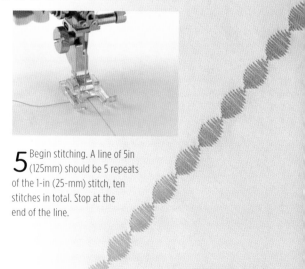

5 Begin stitching. A line of 5in (125mm) should be 5 repeats of the 1-in (25-mm) stitch, ten stitches in total. Stop at the end of the line.

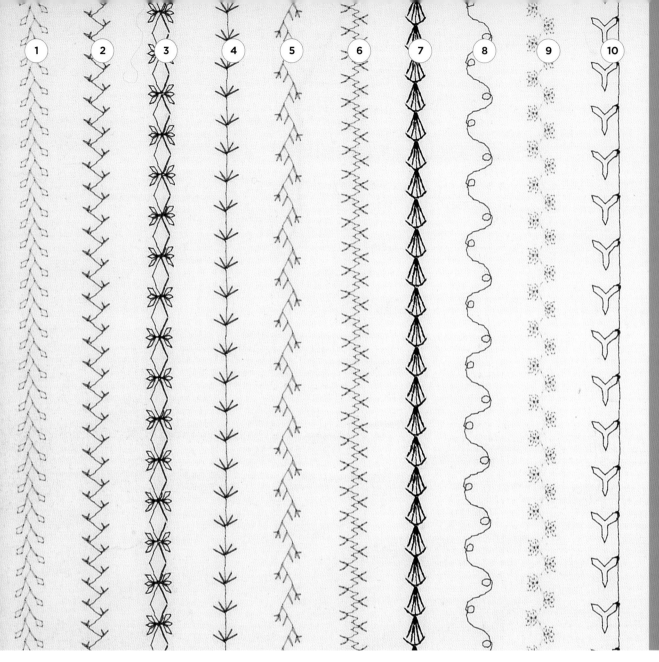

Decorative

Quilting decorative (1) $^3/_8$in *(9mm) wide:* This stitch is good for decorating quilts and crazy patchwork. Use over seam lines on patchwork projects.

Quilting decorative (2) $^3/_8$in *(9mm) wide:* This stitch can be used to sew over seams to decorate patchwork and quilting.

Decorative (3) $^3/_8$in *(9mm) wide:* A double-sided decorative stitch. To make this stitch more pronounced, use a 30-weight thread in the top and bobbin.

Decorative (4) $^5/_{16}$in *(8mm) wide:* This stitch is similar in appearance to a hand-embroidered fly stitch. Use with other rows of stitches as a filler.

Decorative (5) $^3/_8$in *(9mm) wide:* Sew parallel rows just touching each other in opposite directions with this stitch to create a decorated piece of fabric for use in other projects.

Decorative (6) $^3/_8$in *(9mm) wide:* This stitch has an open V either side of a running stitch and is great for stitching over two narrow rows of ribbon.

Decorative (7) $^1/_4$in *(7mm) wide:* As this stitch has a heavy appearance, it is good for stitching on thicker braids.

Decorative (8) $^3/_8$in *(9mm) wide:* A light and open decorative stitch that is suitable for thinner fabrics.

Decorative (9) $^3/_8$in *(9mm) wide:* A small-leafed flower sits evenly on both sides of the stitch. Use on delicate fabrics.

Russian chain (10) $^3/_8$in *(9mm) wide:* A simulation of a hand-embroidered Russian chain stitch. Choose a thicker thread to emulate hand embroidery.

Floral (11) $^3/_8$in *(9mm) wide:* Delicate little flowers are suitable for lightweight fabrics. If both sides of the fabric are to be on view—for example, a border on a voile curtain—use the same color embroidery thread in the bobbin.

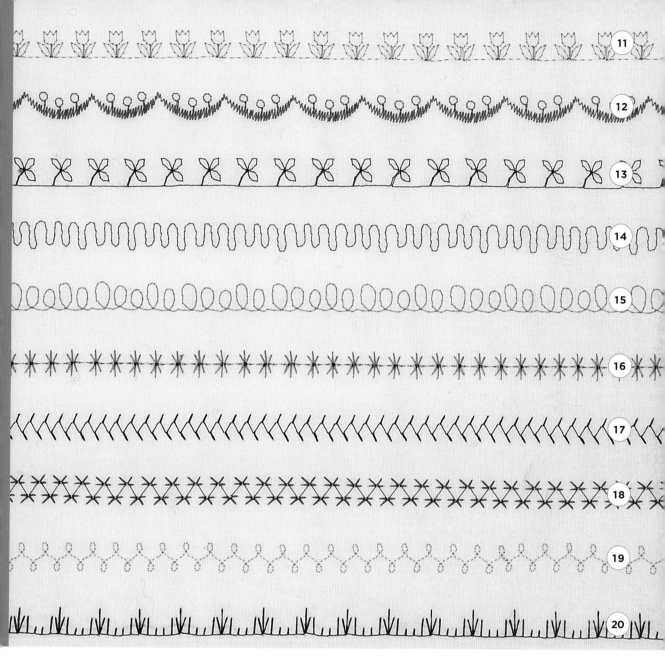

Satin-edged scallop (12) $^{3}/_{8}$in (9mm) *wide:* The satin edge of this stitch can be trimmed back to produce a pretty scalloped edging. Use a fray-stopping product to prevent the stitches from raveling.

Decorative leaves (13) $^{3}/_{8}$in (9mm) *wide:* This delicate leaf design works well on hems, cuffs, and over seam lines in quilting projects. This stitch can also be used in quilting to decorate the surface of blocks or to highlight seam lines.

Quilting stipple (14) $^{3}/_{8}$in (9mm) *wide:* This stitch is used for densely quilting around motifs to bring the motif into relief. A walking foot can be used.

Quilting swirl (15) $^{3}/_{8}$in (9mm) *wide:* These are used to quilt through three layers around motifs. A walking foot can be used.

Linked asterisk (16) $^{3}/_{8}$in (9mm) *wide:* This stitch is used in heirloom sewing and as a decorative star border. It is often used with a metallic thread.

Patchwork (17) $^{3}/_{8}$in (9mm) *wide:* This stitch is used to create a handmade look on patchwork. Use thicker 30-weight thread for a more pronounced look.

Decorative (18) $^{3}/_{8}$in (9mm) *wide:* This stitch is used in quilting to decorate the surface of blocks or to highlight crazy patches along seam lines.

Looped stitch (19) $^{3}/_{8}$in (9mm) *wide:* Looped stitch is used for decorative work on quilted seams. The smaller the stitch, the closer together the loops.

Decorative arrows (20) $^{3}/_{8}$in (9mm) *wide:* Decorative arrows with a running-stitch base are a good stitch for decorating the edges of hems or down the front of button panels.

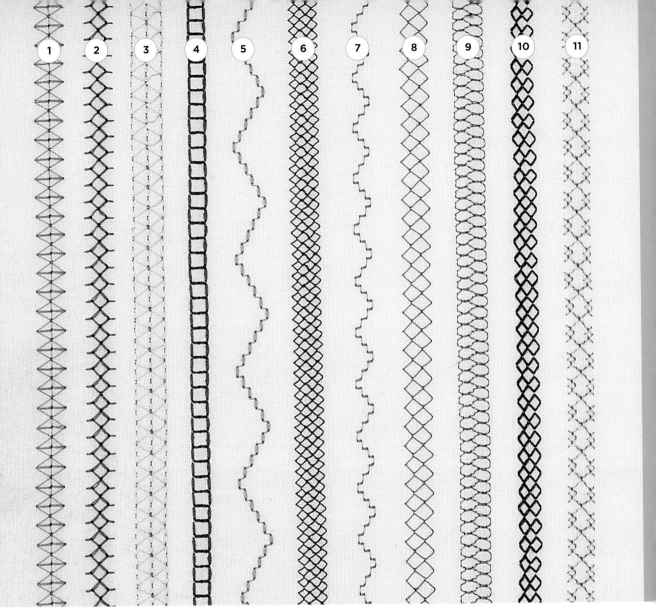

Heirloom

Hemstitch (1) $^3/_8in$ (9mm) wide: Used to decorate the hemmed edges of household linens. The decorative stitch can be stitched with embroidery thread or cotton for a more hand-stitched decoration.

Hemstitch (2) $^1/_4in$ (6mm) wide: This stitch can be sewn over drawn threads or as embellishment for traditional home décor and ladies' and children's clothes.

Hemstitch (3) $^3/_8in$ (9mm) wide: A wider hemstitch with a running-stitch edge that can be used to stitch on a folded hem to hold the layers together decoratively.

Double ladder stitch (4) $^1/_4in$ (5mm) wide: This stitch is used to hold flat seams together. Each stitch is sewn twice to make the stitch prominent.

Smocking stitch (5) $^3/_8in$ (9mm) wide Argyle: This stitch is used to decorate smocking. The smocking is created by hand and the smocking stitch is sewn over the pleats to hold them in place.

Smocking stitch (6) $^5/_{16}in$ (8mm) wide honeycomb: Use this stitch to decorate gathers in rows across a smocked bodice. Make the smocked piece before cutting the bodice pattern section out.

Smocking stitch (7) $^3/_8in$ (9mm) wide: This stitch is a smaller smocking stitch more commonly used for children's and babies' clothes.

Open smocking stitch (8) $^3/_8in$ (9mm) wide: This stitch is a more open, less decorative version of honeycomb. Use this stitch on traditional baby heirloom garments.

Sand stitch (9) $^1/_4in$ (6mm) wide: Sand stitch or closed honeycomb is used for creating decorative, slightly raised areas. Stitching in small rounds close together creates a "rise" in the center of each stitch.

Cross stitch (10) $^1/_4in$ (7mm) wide: Two layers of decorative machine cross stitch. Perfect to add borders to samplers and other simple cross-stitch projects.

Cross stitch (11) $^5/_{16}in$ (8mm) wide: Another variation of cross stitch, this one is less dense and perfect for stitching onto linen for borders.

Scallop jewel (12) *³/₈in (9mm) wide:* Scallop stitches are used to create decorative edgings. Playing with the upper or lower tension will pull on the fabric to create texture.

Scallop (13) *³/₈in (9mm) wide:* This stitch is another variation of a scallop. Use on edgings and to decorate clothes.

Scallop (14) *¹/₄in (6mm) wide:* This is the same stitch as above, reduced to ¹/₄in (6mm) wide. Note that the number of stitches is the same but the finished stitch is denser.

Scallop, mirror image (15) *¹/₄in (6mm) wide:* This is the same as the above, but turned to face the other way. Mirror image a stitch and sew it parallel to the first line to create the illusion of a wider stitch.

Decorative Y border (16) *³/₈in (9mm) wide:* Use this stitch as a decoration on the edges of hems and down the front of button closures. It is particularly effective when used with a brightly colored, 30-weight thread on children's clothes.

Decorative honeycomb (17) *³/₈in (9mm) wide:* A fancy stitch used for decorating heirloom projects—for example, adjacent to rows of pin tucks.

Insertion stitch (18) *³/₈in (9mm) wide:* Machine insertion stitch is used to stitch two hemmed edges together by sewing from one side to another in a decorative way. Two flat edges are created deliberately in heirloom sewing projects to use insertion stitch in a decorative manner.

Insertion stitch (19) *³/₈in (9mm) wide:* A wider, more open and decorative insertion stitch. This one can be used where the fabric is thicker and you require extra embellishment.

Decorative (20) *³/₈in (9mm) wide:* This is a very delicate decorative stitch used for simple borders or in parallel rows on heirloom projects.

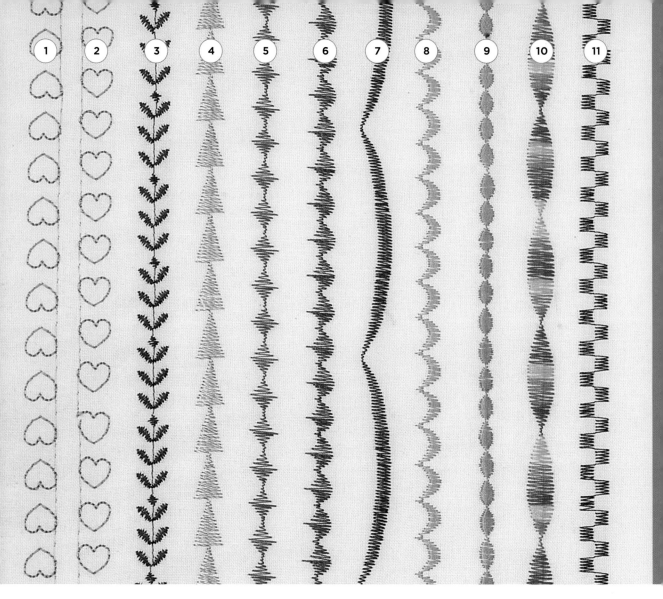

Satin stitches

Satin-edged hearts (1) *³/₈in (9mm) wide:* Over-sew each heart stitch for a pronounced look.

Satin-edged hearts mirrored (2) *³/₈in (9mm) wide:* Sew two rows of the same stitch, mirrored and reversed to create a wider-looking stitch.

Fern leaf stitch (3) *³/₈in (9mm) wide:* A satin-stitched leaf design. Try not to reduce this stitch too much, as the leaves become too dense and distort.

Satin triangles (4) *³/₈in (9mm) wide:* This stitch can be used on borders or stitched onto ribbon to hold it in place.

Satin diamonds (5) *³/₈in (9mm) wide:* This stitch can be reduced to create a thicker, denser stitch or enlarged to make an open, long diamond shape. The longer the stitch, the less dense it is.

Satin scallop (6) *³/₈in (9mm) wide:* This stitch makes a stunning border. If it is reduced, the density increases. Trim away excess fabric after sewing for a scalloped edge.

Scalloped border (7) *³/₈in (9mm) wide, length x 5, stitch density default 0.40:* This is the scalloped border set to its widest and longest. The stitch can be trimmed back after sewing to create a pretty edge.

Scalloped border (8) *⁵/₁₆in (8mm) wide, length x 1, stitch density 0.30:* This is the same stitch set to the default length, but with the satin stitches set to a density of 0.30. This means that the spacing between the stitches is small, creating a much denser stitch.

Satin-stitch beads (9) *¹/₄in (5mm) wide, length x 1, stitch density 0.20:* A small, tight beading stitch. These are quite difficult to sew over, so a foot with a channel underneath is useful.

Longer satin-stitch beads (10) *³/₈in (9mm) wide, length x 2, stitch density 0.50:* A longer, looser, and less tightly stitched satin-stitch bead.

Cording (11) *³/₈in (9mm) wide:* Use cording stitches to hold down ribbons, cords, and braids. Feed the ribbon, cord, or braid under the foot slowly and evenly.

Long decorative stitch (12) $^3/_8$in (9mm) *wide:* This long stitch is made up of two sections. Watch out for the length when marking out rows.

Short open club stitch (13) $^3/_8$in (9mm) *wide:* The club stitch can be open or filled with satin stitches. Choose the orientation and width before you begin the row.

Satin-filled heart (14) $^1/_4$in (7mm) *wide:* The satin heart is a very popular stitch. Slow the machine down and feed the fabric carefully to keep all the hearts uniform in size and shape.

Satin hearts programmed with lettering (15) $^3/_8$in (9mm) *wide lettering,* $^3/_8$in (9mm) *wide hearts:* Program three hearts and then the lettering. Select Repeat to continue the design. This can be saved to the memory in a computerized sewing machine.

Spiral satin stitch (16) $^3/_8$in (9mm) *wide:* Fabric needs to be fed slowly through the machine so that the stitch is formed evenly. Use a foot with a channel underneath for optimum results.

Curly open leaf (17) $^5/_{16}$in (8mm) *wide:* This stitch is classed as a satin stitch because the centers of the leaves have tiny satin stitches. Try to keep this stitch at default, otherwise the stitches in the center of the leaf may distort.

Decorative (18) $^3/_8$in (9mm) *wide:* This stitch is lovely on geometric and contemporary projects.

Star designs (19) $^3/_8$in (9mm) *wide:* The star is another popular stitch. When the machine stitches the shape, the fabric moves quickly in different directions, so go slowly to enable you to keep your eyes on the sewing line.

Closed-leaf scroll (20) $^3/_8$in (9mm) *wide:* This stitch has full satin-stitched leaves. Be careful about resizing, as the satin stitches in the leaves become too close together if the stitch is reduced too far. Use on borders or to decorate delicate fabrics such as voile or chiffon. When sewing on a delicate fabric, use a water-soluble stabilizer and wash it out afterward.

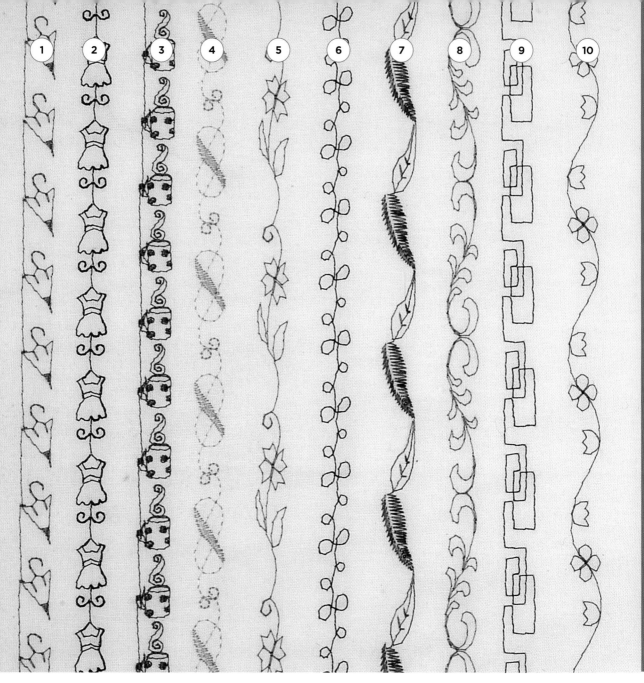

Picture, play, or long stitch

These stitches are named in some sewing machines as long, picture, or play stitches. They can be used to decorate all manner of items, from borders on children's clothes through to quilting and patchwork projects.

Stitch orientation

Take a close look at the way these stitches are sewn out and practice before beginning a project. Whether they are pictured going down or across, all are stitched downward and, if the project requires them to be sewn across, it should be turned afterward.

Fabric movement

The fabric moves a lot when these stitches are sewn. If your machine can sew these decorative stitches it will have omni-motion, which means it can feed left and right as well as up and down. Let the fabric move in the direction it wants to and just hold it to keep it steady. As each stitch forms, the machine will return to the center point. Keep an eye on the center line between stitches to keep it on a straight line.

Fabric stabilizing

Use a good-quality tearaway stabilizer or batting and a bottom layer of fabric underneath the main fabric in a three-layer sandwich for quilting. If you sew decorative stitches onto a delicate fabric—for example, chiffon—or for heirloom work on fine cotton, you

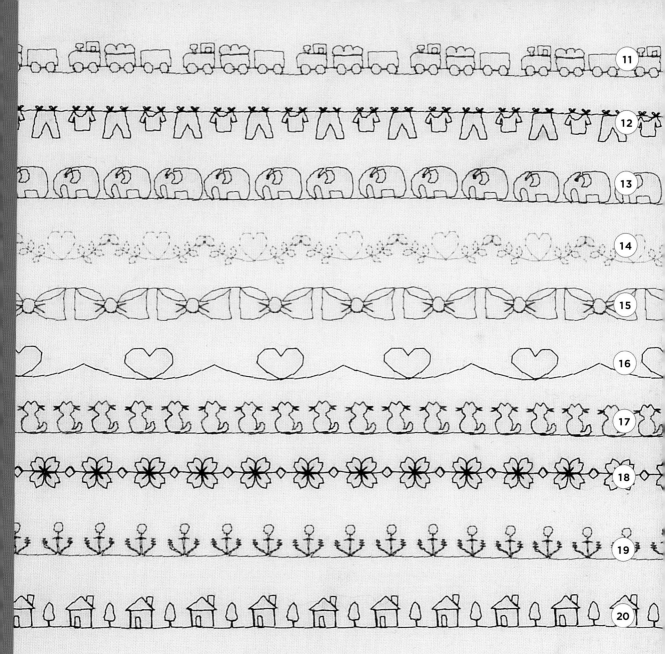

can use a water-soluble stabilizer underneath the fabric and wash it away afterward. If you are quilting, a walking foot helps to feed the layers evenly.

Resizing the stitches
Most of these stitches can be resized. However, they are put into the machines at optimum size, so resizing can distort them if used above 20 percent in either direction.

Thread choices
Make the most of the thread choices available. A brightly colored space-dyed thread looks superb when a children's stitch is selected. A thicker 30-weight thread makes all the stitches more prominent. Use a thread doubled with two of the same or two different colors for a lovely look. A twisted thread gives depth to the stitches and a variegated thread spreads different colors through the design.

Stitch names and categories
Umbrella: play stitch (1)
Mannequin: play stitch (2)
Coffee cup: play stitch (3)
Scroll: long stitch (4)
Flower: long stitch (5)
Curly simple: long stitch (6)
Double leaf: long stitch (7)
Triple leaf: long stitch (8)
Contemporary square: long stitch (9)
Flower and small tulip: long stitch (10)
Train and carriages: picture stitch (11)
Washing line: picture stitch (12)
Elephants: picture stitch (13)
Hearts and leaves: picture stitch (14)
Ribbon bows: picture stitch (15)
Hearts and scallops: picture stitch (16)
Cute cats: picture stitch (17)
Flower and diamond: picture stitch (18)
Anchor: picture stitch (19)
House and tree: picture stitch (20)

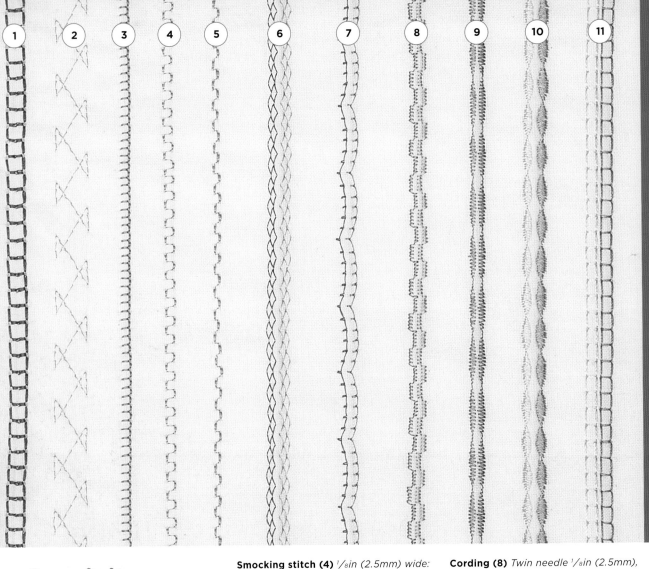

Specialty attachments

WING NEEDLE SIZE 100

Simple swing stitches work best with wing needles.

Double ladder stitch (1) *¹/₄in (5mm) wide:* This stitch is widely used in heirloom sewing.

Insertion stitch with wing needle (2) *³/₈in (9mm) wide:* This wider, more open, and decorative insertion stitch is good with a wing needle.

Appliqué stitch (3) *¹/₈in (3mm) wide appliqué stitch with a wing needle:* This stitch swings back and forth twice over the edge of fabric for appliqué. It makes a good decorative wing-needle stitch without the appliqué fabric.

Smocking stitch (4) *¹/₈in (2.5mm) wide:* The wing needle sews over each stitch twice, thus making the decorative holes cleaner and more visible to the eye.

Smocking stitch (5) *¹/₈in (2mm) wide:* This stitch is kept narrow to show off even wing-needle stitches. If it is too wide, the stitch may look clumsy.

TWIN NEEDLES

The narrower the spacing on the twin needles, the closer the rows of stitching.

Smocking stitch (6) *Twin needle size ¹/₈in (4mm), stitch width ¹/₈in (3mm), stitch length ¹/₈in (2.5mm). This stitch is also known as Grandmother's Garden. It produces two rows of diamonds.*

Scallops (7) *Twin needle size ¹/₈in (3mm), stitch width ¹/₈in (3mm), stitch length ¹/₈in (2.5mm). This single-stitch scallop has been elongated to produce two rows of gently tapering stitches.*

Cording (8) *Twin needle ¹/₈in (2.5mm), stitch width ¹/₈in (2.5mm), stitch length 0.4mm. When used with an ¹/₈-in (2.5-mm) twin needle, the stitches are too narrow to stitch over ribbon.*

Decorative beading (9) *Twin needle ¹/₈in (2.5mm), stitch width ¹/₈in (2mm), stitch length 0.4mm. The beading stitch has been lengthened so it tapers more gently. Each individual bead has less density.*

Decorative beading (10) *Twin needle size ¹/₈in (4mm), stitch width ¹/₈in (3mm), stitch length 0.3mm. This beading stitch has been shortened, which makes the stitching dense and more prominent.*

Ladder stitch (11) *Twin needle size ¹/₈in (4mm), stitch width ¹/₈in (3mm), stitch length ¹/₈in (5mm). As ladder stitch sews each stitch twice, two rows using different colors are very effective.*

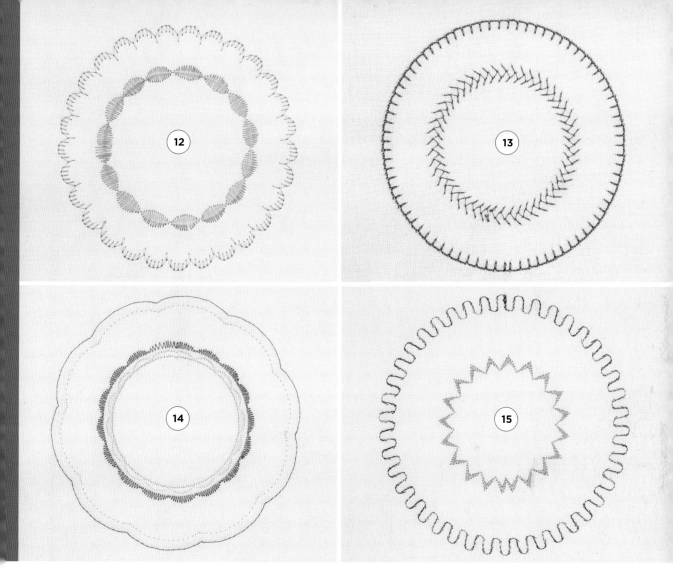

CIRCLES WITH CIRCULAR ATTACHMENT

Circle (12) *Outer circle:* Diameter 3½in (9cm), distance from needle 1¾in (4.5cm), stitch width ¼in (7mm), stitch length ⅛in (2.5mm).
Scallop: The same scallop as used in the twin-needle sewing has been reduced to create a deeper curve.
Inner circle: Diameter 2¼in (6cm), distance from needle 1¼in (3cm), stitch width ¼in (7mm), stitch length 0.7mm.
Beading: The beading stitch has been set to create a bigger bead without too much density.

Circle (13) *Outer circle:* Diameter 3½in (9cm), distance from needle 1¾in (4.5cm), wing needle size 100, stitch width ⅛in (3.5mm), stitch length ⅛in (2.5mm).
Parisian stitch: This stitch is used extensively with a wing needle for heirloom sewing. The stitch goes over

each section twice with the thread, so the needle penetrates each hole twice, giving a nice crisp look.
Inner circle: Diameter 2¼in (6cm), distance from needle 1¼in (3cm), wing needle size 100, stitch width ¼in (5mm), stitch length ⅛in (3.5mm).
Briar stitch: This stitch is a good choice for a wing needle, as it is simple.

Circle (14) *Outer circle:* Diameter 4in (10cm), distance from needle 2in (5cm), twin needle size ⅛in (4mm), stitch width ⅛in (3mm), stitch length ⅛in (2.5mm).
Scallop single stitch: The parallel rows of straight stitch make a good choice for twin needles.
Inner circle: Diameter 2¼in (6cm), distance from needle 1¼in (3cm), twin needle size ⅛in (4mm), stitch width ⅛in (3mm), stitch length 0.7mm.
Satin scallop: This satin scallop is stitched at default width, but only very

slightly increased in length from the default setting to allow it to feed more smoothly for circular sewing.

Circle (15) *Outer circle:* Diameter 4in (10cm), distance from needle 2in (5cm), stitch width ¼in (7mm), stitch length 1in (2.5cm).
Decorative swirl: This simple stitch looks very effective when a variegated thread is used. Several rows close together can be used for quilting.
Inner circle: Diameter 2in (5cm), distance from needle 1in (2.5cm), stitch width ¼in (7mm), stitch length 0.5mm.
Decorative triangle: Small satin-stitched triangles linked together. This is a very good border stitch.

Common problems and their remedies

Occasionally, things can go wrong. Over the next few pages, you will find a collection of the more common problems and ways to remedy them. Follow through the lists given, checking everything, aiming to be patient with yourself and your machine.

Top thread is tangled
- Upper thread is not threaded correctly. Stop the machine and re-thread from the beginning.
- Wrong needle or thread for selected fabric. Check the needle/thread/fabric combinations.

Upper thread is too tight
- The bobbin is not inserted correctly. Remove the bobbin and replace, ensuring that the thread is correctly pulled through the tension.
- Upper thread has caught on the thread spool. Look at the top threading and re-thread from the beginning.

Thread tension is incorrect
- Check the upper threading. Re-thread and try again.
- Check the bobbin and follow the correct steps for bobbin insertion. Check that the bobbin is wound evenly.
- Check that the presser foot/ embroidery foot is attached correctly.
- Check the upper thread tension.
- Check the bobbin thread tension.
- Replace the needle with a new one and try again.

Upper thread breaks
- The upper thread is not threaded correctly. Use the correct spool pin, a thread stand, a thread net, thread felt, and double-check to see if the thread is catching anywhere.
- Check the needle. The needle may be blunt, burred, or bent. The needle may not be inserted correctly. Change the needle and insert properly. The wrong needle may be inserted. Check the needle and thread/ fabric combinations. Most problems of upper-thread breakages are with the needle.
- Scratches/burrs on the bobbin case or needle plate. Look at both of these: nicks or burrs will catch the upper thread and cause it to break.
- Upper thread tension is too strong. Thread will break if the upper tension is too tight, so loosen the tension.
- Old or poor-quality thread. Thread ages and will begin to break when it becomes brittle. Cheaper thread isn't strong enough for high speeds. Change the upper thread and try again.
- Twisted threads. The thread may be twisted coming off the spool, or there may be small bits of thread caught in the bobbin area. Remove any stray threads from inside the bobbin area, re-thread, and try again.
- Incorrect bobbin. The bobbin may be incorrect for the machine. Change to the correct bobbin.

Bobbin thread breaks
- The bobbin is not set in correctly. Remove from the bobbin case and insert again, following the manual's guidance for thread direction.
- There are scratches on the bobbin or the bobbin itself is not rotating correctly. Replace the bobbin with a new one and try again. Do not oil modern machines.
- There are loose threads or lint in the bobbin area. Remove the bobbin, the needle plate, and the race, and clean the whole area. Replace them all and start again.

Bobbin thread winding incorrectly or unevenly
- The correct thread paths for bobbin winding are not being followed. Refer to the manual and re-thread.
- Wind the bobbin on a slower speed. Ensure that the bobbin is on the spool correctly.
- Begin the bobbin winding by hand, or make sure that the bobbin thread is pulled through the hole in the top of the bobbin, and held for the first few turns of the bobbin before trimming.

Skipped or missed stitches
- The needle may be burred, bent, or dull. The needle may be the incorrect size or type for the fabric. The needle may be inserted incorrectly.
- The wrong stabilizer is being used. Check the stabilizer choice for your fabric.
- Lint, dust, or thread is caught in the bobbin area. Remove the bobbin, the needle plate, and the race, and clean the whole area. Replace them all and start again.

Needle breaks
Remember, needles break for a reason: stop the machine, because something is wrong.
- The wrong needle is being used. Check needle/fabric/thread combination.
- Needle not inserted correctly. Check the needle clamp and screw, insert the needle correctly.
- The upper thread has caught. This is very common. The upper thread falls off the spool too quickly and gets caught up. Re-thread with a different thread, a different spool, using a thread net or, for cones, use a thread stand.
- The upper thread is too tight. Poor upper tension will pull on the needle and cause it to break. Loosen the upper tension.
- Incorrect threading. If the upper/lower threading is incorrect, the needle will break after the first few stitches. Re-thread both upper and bobbin threads.
- Embroidery is too thick. Some embroidery is poorly digitized. Inexperienced digitizers sew stitches in a pile on top of each other over and over again in layers rather than "cut holes" or "remove overlaps." A good digitizer removes stitches in the bottom layers of an embroidery design. A needle will break if the machine doesn't want to stitch through too many layers of thread. Change the needle, but, if it happens again, change your embroidery design before damaging the motor on your machine.
- Wrong presser foot is used. A needle will break if it hits the presser foot. A needle will break if the wrong stitch is selected for the width allowed by the presser foot and it hits the needle plate.
- Presser foot is loose. A needle will snap if the presser foot/presser foot holder is not attached correctly. Tighten all screws.
- Fabric is pulled, is too thick, or fed forcefully. The fabric should feed smoothly. If it doesn't, make the correct adjustments to pressure, stabilizer, and needle choice, and try again.

Embroidery or fabric puckers
- The fabric is pulled too tightly in the hoop. Re-hoop without distorting or pulling on the grain.
- The incorrect stabilizer is used for the fabric and density of design choice. Look again at the density of the design and choose a stronger stabilizer.
- The fabric wasn't prewashed. Always prewash fabric before embroidery.

- The wrong design was chosen for the fabric being embroidered, so the fabric isn't strong enough to support the embroidery.

Embroidery design doesn't sew out correctly
- The thread is twisted or threaded incorrectly. Re-thread both upper and lower threads.
- Incorrect bobbinfil. Check with your machine manufacturer or your manual to ensure you are using the correct bobbinfil.
- The fabric wasn't held in the embroidery hoop correctly. Re-hoop, remembering to tighten the screws properly, and don't pull on the fabric. Double-check to make sure that the top and bottom hoops are aligned underneath.
- The fabric/stabilizer combination is incorrect. Have another look at fabric/stabilizer and design density combinations.
- Insufficient stabilizer. Stabilizer underneath fabric needs to be larger than the embroidery hoop to support the fabric properly.

▼ Hooping and stabilizing your fabric correctly is vital to machine embroidery success.

The machine makes a noise or the embroidery doesn't stitch properly

- Check to see that the carriage arm can move freely and isn't knocking on a wall or unit. If it is, switch the machine off and move the machine to where the carriage arm can move easily.
- Carriage arm stops and shudders. This can happen when a needle jams in the fabric or breaks. Take note of the stitch number. Switch the machine off and allow it to reset itself. Replace the needle with a new one. Resume the embroidery where you left off.
- Make sure the bobbin area isn't full of dust, lint, or loose threads. The machine will sound noisy if this area is dirty. Remove the bobbin, the needle plate, and the race, clean it all thoroughly, replace it all, and begin again.
- The fabric is too heavy for the carriage arm to move. If the carriage arm is laboring because the fabric is too heavy, change the fabric.
- The upper thread has caught up and the bobbin thread is jammed underneath. The embroidery stops. Take note of the stitch number. Switch off the machine. Do not tug at the embroidery. Slide a long-handled pair of scissors under the hoop without lifting it. Gently snip away at the bobbin thread until you can lift the jammed section of embroidery away. Don't force this; do it slowly and carefully. Remove the embroidery frame when the bobbin thread has been cut away. Turn over the embroidery and remove all loose threads from the underneath. Take out the bobbin, discard this bobbin thread, and wind a new one. Take off the needle plate and remove the race. Remove all loose threads from the whole area. Replace the race, the needle plate, and a newly wound bobbin. Change the needle. Switch on the machine, put the hoop back on, and resume the embroidery where you left off.

Gaps in the embroidery

- The incorrect stabilizer is being used. Gaps in the stitches or a gap on the inside of a design or outline mean that the fabric has pulled in and the stabilizer wasn't strong enough to prevent this. Change to a stronger stabilizer and try again.
- The design was stitched with a tearaway stabilizer and the stabilizer has fallen apart underneath the embroidery, thus the stitches are misaligned. Change to a stronger stabilizer.
- The thread started to break apart and some stitches are thinner before the actual breakage. Stop, re-thread, and go backward using the needle keys to a point before the gaps. Embroider over the gaps again.

Machine refuses to acknowledge an embroidery design

- The embroidery design transferred to the machine is too big for the largest hoop. If this happens, the machine will not recognize the design and you will not be able to find it.
- You have transferred an embroidery design in the incorrect format for your machine to recognize. Your machine will not be able to find it.
- You are looking in the wrong place. Check to ensure that you are looking for the embroidery design in the correct folder of your machine.

Machine says incorrect or wrong hoop

- The embroidery design you are trying to embroider is too big for your selected hoop. Remove the first hoop, alter the hoop size, put the new size on, and try again. Alternatively, edit the embroidery design or design combination to make it smaller.
- If you have inadvertently moved the machine and the embroidery unit has come apart from the main body, the machine will throw up error messages about the hoop size, incorrect hoop attached, or hoop not attached correctly, and will refuse to work. Switch off the machine, allow it to reset, re-attach the embroidery unit, switch it back on, and try again.

Aftercare of your machine embroidery

Having put a lot of time, effort, and money into embroidering the perfect design, it stands to reason that you want to take care of your work afterward.

LAUNDRY

The hottest wash that polyester thread can withstand is 200°F (95°C) degrees. However, washing your embroidery at 85°F (30°C) degrees is always the safest option. The embroidery doesn't alter at all in a cool wash and, should a thread used not be colorfast, the color won't run.

Use fabric conditioner on clothes and freestanding lace to keep them soft.

TUMBLE DRYERS

If possible, hang your embroidery up to drip dry. This is not possible for all clothing items, especially those for children that are washed and worn often. You can tumble-dry embroidery but it will need ironing flat afterward because it does tend to pucker up in the dryer, but a hot iron and steam press soon sorts this out.

PRESSING

Machine embroidery should always be pressed face down on a folded terry towel. This prevents the stitches from being flattened. The iron temperature will depend on the fabric, not the embroidery—remember to take the fabric into consideration when pressing appliqué.

This pressing technique is not practical for heavily laundered items, in which case you won't do any harm to the embroidery by ironing without a terry towel, but you will make the stitches flatter and remove some of the sheen from high-shine polyester threads. This is not the end of the world on a pair of pajamas, but it is for a family heirloom quilt. Think about your requirements for your finished piece and press accordingly.

DRY CLEANING

Machine embroidery can be drycleaned without any problems. The color will stay fast and the fabric won't pucker up.

STORAGE

If you want to store your embroidery—for example, a christening gown—for a long time, wrap it carefully in unperfumed tissue paper and store in a dark place: storing in direct sunlight or bright daylight causes the fabric and threads to disintegrate and fade over time.

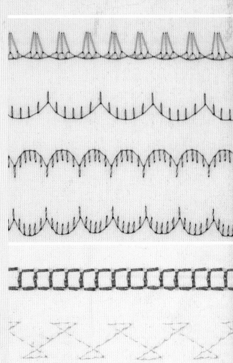

Index

Credits

Quarto would like to thank the following companies for their generous loan of tools, embroidery designs, and equipment:

Bernina, page 96
www.bernina.com

Brother, pages 46 (1), 50 (3,4,5), 58 (3,4,7), 68, 82
www.brothersewing.co.uk

Husqvarna Viking, pages 46 (2) p84, 85(2)
www.husqvarnaviking.com

Janome, page 98
www.janome.com

Pfaff, page 50 (1 and 2)
www.pfaff.com

Quarto would also like to thank the following digitizers for their skills and/or digitized embroidery designs:

A bit of stitch, Evy Hawkins, pages 79 (1), 93 (2), 95 (2)
www.abitofstitch.com

Adorable ideas, John Deer, pages 58 (5), 65, 86
www.adorableideas.com

Anita Goodesign, Steve Wilson, pages 75(2), 83 (1 and 2), 87, 97 (2), 99 (2), 103 (1 and 2), 105 (1)
www.anitagoodesignonline.com

Carolyn Sinclair, page 104

Loveday embroideries, Daniel Loveday, pages 43, 90
www.flairmagazine.co.uk

Elsas's designs, Elsa Goussard, page 72
www.elsasdesigns.com

Embroidershoppe, Zandra Shaw, pages 58 (6), 93 (1)
www.embroidershoppe.com

Embroidery Library, Debra Mundinger, pages 24, 31, 39,58 (2), 79 (2), 91 (1 and 2), 97 (1)
www.emblibrary.com

Enchanting Embroidery, Margarita Kovnat, page 89
www.enchantingembroidery.com

Flair Design collections, Lucy Brandon, pages 94, 96, 100, 102
www.flairmagazine.co.uk

Golden Needle Designs, Keavy Hayes, page 81
www.goldenneedledesigns.com

Graceful Embroidery, Hazel Tunbridge, pages 75(1), 95 (1)
www.gracefulembroidery.com

Hatched in Africa, Santi and Liese Brouwer, pages 74, 92, 99 (1), 101 (2)
www.hatchedinafrica.com

Premium Embroidery, page 58 (1)
www.embroiderydesigns.com

Rachel Espin, page 88

Stitch Delight, Daleen Lubbe, pages 77 (1 and 2), 78, 85, 101 (1), 105 (2)
www.stitchdelight.net

Sudberry House, Ellen Maurer-Stroh, page 80
www.machinecrossstitch.com

Urban Threads, Karline Koehler, pages 73, 76
www.urbanthreads.com

Additional thanks go to: Carolyn Sinclair and George le Warré for help with the software section; Angela and Yvonne from Lords sewing (www.lordsewing.co.uk); Evy, Santi, Liese, Hazel, Deborah, Daleen, Keavy, Lisa, and Karline who provided samples for the

Ideas Files; Jonathon from Barnyarns (www.barnyarns.co.uk) for providing equipment for photography and Princess Embroidery Threads (www.princessembroidery.co.uk) for sending a full collection of embroidery thread; Transcend information (www.transcend-info.com) for the images they sent for page 26.

All step-by-step and other images are the copyright of Quarto Publishing plc. While every effort has been made to credit contributors, Quarto would like to apologize should there have been any omissions or errors—and would be pleased to make the appropriate correction for future editions of the book.

Author's acknowledgements
I would like to thank all the Flair Magazine contributors who have taught me so much over the years, and lastly, I would like to thank my mum, dad, and two daughters for their support.